Cognitive
Therapy

Theories of Psychotherapy Series

Theories of Psychotherapy Series

Jon Carlson and Matt Englar-Carlson, Series Editors

Cognitive Therapy

Keith S. Dobson

American Psychological Association

Washington, DC

Published by   To order
American Psychological Association   APA Order Department
750 First Street, NE   P.O. Box 92984
Washington, DC 20002   Washington, DC 20090-2984
www.apa.org   Tel: (800) 374-2721; Direct: (202) 336-5510
                                                Fax: (202) 336-5502; TDD/TTY: (202) 336-6123

Online: www.apa.org/pubs/books
E-mail: order@apa.org

In the U.K., Europe, Africa, and the Middle East, copies may be ordered from
American Psychological Association
3 Henrietta Street
Covent Garden, London
WC2E 8LU England

Typeset in Minion by Circle Graphics, Columbia, MD

Printer: Maple-Vail Book Manufacturing Group, York, PA
Cover Designer: Minker Design, Sarasota, FL
Cover Art: *Lily Rising,* 2005, oil and mixed media on panel in craquelure frame, by Betsy Bauer

The opinions and statements published are the responsibility of the authors, and such opinions and statements do not necessarily represent the policies of the American Psychological Association.

Library of Congress Cataloging-in-Publication Data

Dobson, Keith S.
  Cognitive therapy / Keith S. Dobson — 1st ed.
    p.; cm. — (Theories of psychotherapy series)
  Includes bibliographical references and index.
  ISBN-13: 978-1-4338-1088-6
  ISBN-10: 1-4338-1088-3
  1. Cognitive therapy. I. American Psychological Association. II. Title. III. Series:
  Theories of psychotherapy series.
  [DNLM: 1. Cognitive Therapy. WM 425.5.C6]
  RC489.C63D64 2012
  616.89'1425—dc23
                                        2011026989

British Library Cataloguing-in-Publication Data
A CIP record is available from the British Library.

Printed in the United States of America
First Edition

Contents

Series Preface

Some might argue that in the contemporary clinical practice of psychotherapy, evidence-based intervention and effective outcome have overshadowed theory in importance. Maybe. But, as the editors of this series, we don't propose to take up that controversy here. We do know that psychotherapists adopt and practice according to one theory or another because their experience, and decades of good evidence, suggests that having a sound theory of psychotherapy leads to greater therapeutic success. Still, the role of theory in the helping process can be hard to explain. This narrative about solving problems helps convey theory's importance:

> Aesop tells the fable of the sun and wind having a contest to decide who was the most powerful. From above the earth, they spotted a man walking down the street, and the wind said that he bet he could get his coat off. The sun agreed to the contest. The wind blew, and the man held on tightly to his coat. The more the wind blew, the tighter he held. The sun said it was his turn. He put all of his energy into creating warm sunshine, and soon the man took off his coat.

What does a competition between the sun and the wind to remove a man's coat have to do with theories of psychotherapy? We think this deceptively simple story highlights the importance of theory as the precursor to any effective intervention—and hence to a favorable outcome. Without a guiding theory we might treat the symptom without understanding the role of the individual. Or we might create power conflicts with our clients and not understand that, at times, indirect means of helping (sunshine) are often as effective—if not more so—than direct ones (wind). In the absence of theory, we might lose track of the treatment rationale and instead get caught up in, for example, social correctness and not wanting to do something that looks too simple.

What exactly *is* theory? The *APA Dictionary of Psychology* defines theory as "a principle or body of interrelated principles that purports to explain or predict a number of interrelated phenomena." In psychotherapy, a theory is a set of principles used to explain human thought and behavior, including what causes people to change. In practice, a theory creates the goals of therapy and specifies how to pursue them. Haley (1997) noted that a theory of psychotherapy ought to be simple enough for the average therapist to understand, but comprehensive enough to account for a wide range of eventualities. Furthermore, a theory guides action toward successful outcomes while generating hope in both the therapist and client that recovery is possible.

Theory is the compass that allows psychotherapists to navigate the vast territory of clinical practice. In the same ways that navigational tools have been modified to adapt to advances in thinking and ever-expanding territories to explore, theories of psychotherapy have changed over time. The different schools of theories are commonly referred to as waves, the first wave being psychodynamic theories (i.e., Adlerian, psychoanalytic), the second wave learning theories (i.e., behavioral, cognitive–behavioral), the third wave humanistic theories (person-centered, gestalt, existential), the fourth wave feminist and multicultural theories, and the fifth wave postmodern and constructivist theories. In many ways, these waves represent how psychotherapy has adapted and responded to changes in psychology, society, and epistemology as well as to changes in the nature of psychotherapy itself. Psychotherapy and the theories that guide it are dynamic and responsive. The wide variety of theories is also testament to the different ways in which the same human behavior can be conceptualized (Frew & Spiegler, 2008).

It is with these two concepts in mind—the central importance of theory and the natural evolution of theoretical thinking—that we developed the APA Theories of Psychotherapy Series. Both of us are thoroughly fascinated by theory and the range of complex ideas that drive each model. As university faculty members who teach courses on the theories of psychotherapy, we wanted to create learning materials that not only highlight the essence of the major theories for professionals and professionals in training but also clearly bring the reader up to date on the current status of the models. Often in books on theory, the biography of the original theorist overshadows the evolution of the model. In contrast, our intent is to highlight the contemporary uses of the theories as well as their history and context.

As this project began, we faced two immediate decisions: which theories to address and who best to present them. We looked at graduate-level theories of psychotherapy courses to see which theories are being taught, and we explored popular scholarly books, articles, and conferences to determine which theories draw the most interest. We then developed a dream list of authors from among the best minds in contemporary theoretical practice. Each author is one of the leading proponents of that approach as well as a knowledgeable practitioner. We asked each author to review the core constructs of the theory, bring the theory into the modern sphere of clinical practice by looking at it through a context of evidence-based practice, and clearly illustrate how the theory looks in action.

There are 24 titles planned for the series. Each title can stand alone or can be put together with a few other titles to create materials for a course in psychotherapy theories. This option allows instructors to create a course featuring the approaches they believe are the most salient today. To support this end, APA Books has also developed a DVD for each of the approaches that demonstrates the theory in practice with a real client. Many of the DVDs show therapy over six sessions. Contact APA Books for a complete list of available DVD programs (http://www.apa.org/pubs/videos).

Cognitive therapy is easily one of the most popular approaches to psychotherapy today. As one of the approaches within the umbrella of cognitive–behavioral therapies, cognitive therapy emphasizes the role of thinking on behavioral and emotional responses. In *Cognitive Therapy,* Keith S. Dobson carefully takes the reader through a primer on this empirically validated approach. The core concepts of cognitive therapy are paired with client examples to show how this approach looks in actual practice. More importantly, however, Dobson shows the reader how to think like a cognitive therapist so that a theoretically consistent case formulation and conceptualization can be enacted through cognitive technique and interventions. Overall, we really enjoyed Dobson's manner of clearly highlighting a typical course of treatment through a cognitive theoretical model. Though there are many other books about cognitive therapy, we are sure readers will appreciate the clarity of this book.

—Jon Carlson and Matt Englar-Carlson

REFERENCES

Frew, J., & Spiegler, M. (2008). *Contemporary psychotherapies for a diverse world.* Boston, MA: Lahaska Press.

Haley, J. (1997). *Leaving home: The therapy of disturbed young people.* New York, NY: Routledge.

How to Use This Book
With APA Psychotherapy Videos

Each book in the Theories of Psychotherapy Series is specifically paired with a DVD that demonstrates the theory applied in actual therapy with a real client. Many DVDs feature the author of the book as the guest therapist, allowing students to see eminent scholars and practitioners putting the theory they write about into action.

The DVDs have a number of features that make them useful for learning more about theoretical concepts:

- Many DVDs contain six full sessions of psychotherapy over time, giving viewers a chance to see how clients respond to the application of the theory over the course of several sessions.
- Each DVD has a brief introductory discussion recapping the basic features of the theory behind the approach demonstrated. This allows viewers to review the key aspects of the approach about which they have just read.
- DVDs feature actual clients in unedited psychotherapy sessions. This provides an opportunity to get a sense of the look and feel of real psychotherapy, something that written case examples and transcripts sometimes cannot convey.
- There is a therapist commentary track that viewers may choose to play during the psychotherapy sessions. This track gives insight into why therapists do what they do in a session. Further, it provides an in vivo opportunity to see how the therapist uses the model to conceptualize the client.

The books and DVDs together make a powerful teaching tool for showing how theoretical principles affect practice. In the case of this book, the DVD *Cognitive Therapy Over Time* features author Keith S. Dobson as the guest expert who provides a vivid example of what cognitive therapy looks like in practice. In the six sessions featured on this DVD, Dobson works with a woman in her late 30s who presents with a number of health- and anxiety-related concerns and whose primary concern, related to panic attacks, becomes the focus of therapy. Over the course of therapy, Dobson begins by assessing the nature of the panic disorder, and her anxiety in general, and then works with the client to reduce the frequency of panic attacks. The primary interventions demonstrated in the DVD include in-session panic induction, between-session homework, and cognitive restructuring.

Acknowledgments

Since my graduation in 1980, it has been my privilege to work with a multitude of inquisitive, devoted, critical (in the best sense of the word), and companionable colleagues in the field of cognitive therapy. Brian Shaw was an early influence, and he provided a number of connections within the field, including Aaron Beck and others at the University of Pennsylvania. Over the years I have had the opportunity to talk, collaborate, socialize, and "conspire" with a number of "movers and shakers" from many countries, including Neil Jacobson, Steve Hollon, Sona Dimidjian, Phil Kendall, Zindel Segal, John Teasdale, Bob Leahy, Jeff Young, Jackie Persons, Judy Beck, Leslie Sokol, Robert DeRubeis, Maureen Whitall, Willem Kuyken, Ed Watkins, Ladan Fata, Mehmet Sungur, Antonella Montano, Sharon Freeman, Nik Kazantsis, and Luis Oswaldo Perez Flores, among many others. It has been fun, to say the least!

I wish to recognize and reciprocate the ongoing love and support of my wife, Debbie, my direct children, Kit and Beth, and my delightfully growing extended family, including Aubrey, Simon, Alexandra, and Clementine. I also want to acknowledge the ongoing support and efforts of the many students with whom I have worked. I don't think that students often feel empowered, but I would like you to know that you push and inspire me to learn more, to clarify my thinking, and to try and inspire you to be your best. It has been my privilege to work with many students at the University of Calgary and to mentor and support students and trainees from other countries, including Iran, Hong Kong, South Korea, and the United States.

No book exists without the support of many people. This volume is part of the APA Theories of Psychotherapy series, and I want to thank Jon Carlson and Ed Meidenbauer, in particular, for their support and encouragement. I hope that this volume will encourage readers to learn more about cognitive therapy and that you will be able to take what you read and convert that knowledge into support for people who struggle with mental health problems.

Cognitive
Therapy

1

Introduction

Cognitive therapy is without a doubt one of the most successful of the psychotherapies. This success can be observed in terms of the established influence and evidence base for this approach to psychotherapy (Cook, Biyanova, & Coyne, 2009; Epp & Dobson, 2010), the prevalence of cognitive therapy training in graduate and professional programs (Norcross, Hedges, & Prochaska, 2002; M. M. Weissman et al., 2006), and the recent recognition of cognitive therapy as an established therapy by major mental health agencies around the world. For example, Norcross and colleagues (2002) conducted a survey of graduate programs in the United States and discovered that the first- and second-ranked therapies for training in the first decades of the new century were cognitive therapy and the cognitive–behavioral therapies, respectively.

A number of factors have conspired to advance cognitive therapy to its strong position in the mental health field. One is the timing of its emergence: Behavior therapy had reached its zenith in the evolution of psychology and psychiatry, and its influence was beginning to fade. Questions existed about the important role of cognition in behavior change (Mahoney,

1974). Social learning models (Bandura, 1977, 1986) implicated observational, attentional, and memory processes that could not be accommodated in a traditional behavioral framework. Increasingly, evidence emerged that did not fit easily into a behavioral framework.

Cognitive therapy emerged out of the area of clinical depression in the works of A. T. Beck and colleagues (e.g., A. T. Beck, Rush, Shaw, & Emery, 1979). The cognitive model of psychopathology has led to the use of cognitive therapy in the treatment of the full range of anxiety disorders, relational problems, personality disorders, anger, psychosis, and eating disorders, among others.

Another reason for the advancement of cognitive therapy has been the broader movement toward evidence-based practice in health care (American Psychological Association, 2006; Barlow, 1996). The public has long sought treatments that have an evidence base to support them, and there have been legislative and judicial rulings supporting this emphasis. For example, in the United States the Food and Drug Administration has set standards for the development, testing, and deployment of food additives and drugs, due to the perceived public risk if these compounds were not properly and safely developed and marketed. The field of medicine has also broadly adopted the methodology of the randomized clinical trial to ensure that surgical and other medical procedures demonstrate efficacy in the treatment of clinical problems or syndromes. No doubt, part of the movement toward evidence-based medicine is cost-effectiveness: the provision of the most effective and least costly alternative for a given health problem or disorder with minimal risk to patients. Given its relatively time-limited and symptom-focused nature, cognitive therapy also fits well within the movement toward evidence-based practice, or what, in the context of psychotherapy, have been called *empirically supported therapies* (Chambless, 1999; Chambless & Hollon, 1998; Chambless & Ollendick, 2001; K. S. Dobson & Craig, 1998). Standards and procedures for the use of randomized clinical trials in psychotherapy continue to develop (Nezu & Nezu, 2008).

Yet another factor that has assisted in the development of cognitive therapy and empirically supported therapies more generally has been the evolution of diagnostic systems. The *Diagnostic and Statistical Manual of*

Mental Disorders (4th ed.; *DSM–IV*; American Psychiatric Association, 2000) relies on descriptive features of disorders rather than imputed causal factors that might underlie these problems. This descriptive system of diagnosis has, in turn, enabled the development of treatment technologies that do not have a preexisting theoretical link to the disorder's putative theoretical model. Put otherwise, the *DSM–IV* has permitted the possibility that any treatment model might work for any given disorder, but whether it does has become an empirical question. The evidence that cognitive therapy has benefits for a wide range of disorders is mounting.

In summary, a confluence of several factors, including an expansion of behavioral therapies to include cognitive components, research methods that enabled the investigation of the efficacy of psychotherapy, a descriptive diagnostic system, public demand for effective and efficient evidence-based health care, and supportive research evidence, has led to the rapid acceptance and expansion of cognitive therapy as a model of psychotherapy. The past 2 decades have seen an explosion of applications of cognitive therapy approaches.

PREVIEW OF THIS VOLUME

This volume presents the core elements of cognitive therapy, in particular as developed and taught by Beck and colleagues. Chapter 2 gives a brief history of cognitive therapy. Chapter 3 focuses on the cognitive model of psychopathology and how this model is translated into a model of psychotherapy. The contextual factors associated with the therapy are first described, as these factors form the background for delivery of cognitive therapy. Chapter 4, which is by far the longest component of this work, provides a comprehensive survey of the cognitive therapy process, beginning with the typical early processes in cognitive therapy (including intake assessment and case formulation) that provide direction to the course that treatment follows. Subsequent sections of Chapter 4 detail several common cognitive therapy interventions and give examples. The latter sections of Chapter 4 present variations in these techniques for several disorders, although the wide range of applications precludes a complete description of all possible uses of cognitive therapy. The final section of the chapter discusses the processes associated with ending cognitive therapy. Chapter 5 offers a critical assessment of cognitive therapy, and Chapter 6 briefly describes remaining issues for the field. Chapter 7 wraps up this work with a convenient summary.

This volume has been written to be accessible to a wide range of readers, including trainees for whom this is the first exposure to the cognitive therapy and patients[1] who want to understand more about this treatment approach. Where feasible, supplementary sources, and especially more specialized materials for specific topics and disorders, are named so that the interested reader can continue exploring these themes.

---

[1] I use the word *patient* throughout this book to connote that cognitive therapy is most often applied in a mental or physical health setting with people who meet *DSM* criteria for a mental disorder or diagnostic criteria for a medical disorder. Other books use the term *client*, which can be substituted in most cases, if the reader wishes.

2

History

A ttendant to the incorporation of cognitive processes in models of behavior change, the late 1970s saw the emergence of cognitive and behavioral therapy methods, or what was called at that time *cognitive behavior modification* (D. Meichenbaum, 1977). These approaches typically had the goal of observable behavior change, but the techniques to invoke that change sometimes employed cognitive interventions. Also at this time, more formal outlets to share these studies and research results emerged, including the formation of the Association for the Advancement of Behavior Therapy in 1977 and the 1977 launch of a new journal titled *Cognitive Therapy and Research*, under the editorship of Michael Mahoney.

Into the above set of paradigmatic changes came what many saw as an outstanding research result. In a National Institute of Mental Health (NIMH)-funded clinical research trial, which directly contrasted the efficacy of cognitive therapy for depression (A. T. Beck, Rush, Shaw, & Emery, 1979) with a well-established antidepressant medication, the two therapies were reported to have equal outcomes (Rush, Beck, Kovacs, & Hollon, 1977). Furthermore, the 1-year follow-up results yielded a nonsignificant advantage in favor of cognitive therapy (Kovacs, Rush, Beck, & Hollon, 1981). These results were received with great enthusiasm in the emerging world of cognitive–behavioral therapy (CBT) but with great skepticism in the psychiatric world.

Results from the research on cognitive therapy of depression were viewed as so critical to the field, and so controversial, that NIMH replicated and extended the study. The NIMH Treatment of Depression Collaborative Research Program (TDCRP; Elkin et al., 1989) was simultaneously conducted at three sites in the United States, coordinated by a central group of investigators, in an effort to control for possible allegiance effects. It contrasted the short- and long-term effects of cognitive therapy, a second psychotherapy, interpersonal psychotherapy (IPT; Klerman, Weissman, Rounsaville, & Chevron, 1984), and a more contemporary antidepressant medication. The three active therapies were found not to be significantly different in terms of short- or long-term effects on depression (Elkin et al., 1989; Sotsky et al., 1991). These results were not dependent on many initial patient characteristics (Sotsky et al., 1991), but they were mitigated by an interaction with initial depression severity, such that patients who received cognitive therapy but were more depressed at the start of the trial on average did less well than patients who received the other treatments (Elkin et al., 1995). In a later reanalysis of the data from the TDCRP study, an interaction also emerged among the three treatment sites, which led to speculation that the settings with more competent cognitive therapists, IPT therapists, or pharmacotherapists had better results for their respective treatments (Jacobson & Hollon, 1996). In any event, the TDCRP did help to confirm the efficacy of cognitive therapy in the treatment of depression.

Although the cognitive therapy model may have begun in the area of clinical depression, it certainly did not remain there. One of the features of cognitive therapy is that it rests on a cognitive model of psychopathology, a model that is broad enough to allow the conceptualization of other disorders. In this regard, A. T. Beck and Emery (1985) developed a cognitive therapy model and set of interventions for anxiety, and their book was followed by other cognitive therapy books in the domains of relationships (A. T. Beck, 1988), personality disorders (A. T. Beck, Freeman, & David,

2004; Young, 1990), anger (A. T. Beck, 1999), and psychosis (A. T. Beck, Rector, Stolar, & Grant, 2009), among others. Cognitive models have now been advanced for the full range of anxiety disorders (Antony & Swinson, 2000), as well as eating disorders (Fairburn, 2008).

Some of the above treatment models and interventions were clearly ahead of the treatment outcome literature, and in some cases the development of the treatments spurred the advance of treatment research or was part of a program of theory development that then led to outcome research. It is notable, however, that in the development of cognitive therapy there has been a moderately close relationship between the treatment models and efficacy research. Furthermore, as research was conducted either to support or to refute aspects of the model, the treatments were modified. For example, it has long been recognized that people with anxiety disorders are vigilant about their fear and catastrophize about the meaning of confronting their fear. Exposure to the fear situation or object has been recognized as a feature of effective treatment for anxiety disorders for a long time (Antony & Swinson, 2000; Wolpe, 1969). However, research on cognitive aspects of anxiety led to a recognition of safety mechanisms that patients sometimes use (either behavioral or cognitive) and that can maintain fears (Salkovskis, 1989). The elimination of safety mechanisms has now been incorporated into cognitive models and treatments for many anxiety problems (Woody & Rachman, 1994).

COGNITIVE THERAPY AND COGNITIVE–BEHAVIORAL THERAPIES

One of the most deceptively simple questions asked concerns the relationship between cognitive therapy and CBT, or whether there is even a meaningful difference. This question belies the dominant role of cognitive therapy in the larger world of CBT. For most theorists, CBT is the larger or more comprehensive of the two approaches (K. S. Dobson & Dozois, 2010). CBT grew out of behavior therapy and social learning theory but has expanded dramatically over the years to include a variety of specific models and approaches. The field of CBT includes cognitive therapy, rational emotive behavior therapy (Ellis & Whitely, 1979), stress inoculation training (D. H. Meichenbaum & Deffenbacher, 1988), self-instructional training (D. H. Meichenbaum & Jaremko, 1983), problem-solving therapy (D'Zurilla & Nezu, 2007), dialectical behavior therapy (Linehan, 1993), and acceptance and commitment therapy (Fruzzetti & Erikson, 2010; Hayes, Strosahl, & Wilson, 1999), among others. Thus, cognitive therapy is simply one of the CBTs. That said, in many respects cognitive therapy is the preeminent form of CBT. It has the longest tradition of research and outcome studies to support it. It is the CBT model that has been applied to the broadest range of clinical disorders. Cognitive therapy is also a highly adaptable model and can incorporate new techniques with perhaps the greatest ease among the CBTs. Perhaps most important in this regard, cognitive therapy is really a *system* of psychotherapy rather than a set of skills or techniques, and as such it represents a treatment approach rather than any one specific manual or treatment book. Within the current volume, reference will be made to cognitive therapy as a more specific approach than CBT in general. Where this distinction is not possible, that point will be clearly made.

3

Theory

It has been argued that cognitive therapy is based on a *realist* model of human functioning (Held, 1995). According to this model, events occur in the real world, irrespective of whether someone perceives their occurrence and whether they are perceived accurately. From this epistemological underpinning, it can be argued that human adjustment is reflected by optimal accuracy in perception of the world, and by implication, human maladjustment is reflected by lack of accurate correspondence between perception and actual events—or by misperception of the world. Consistent with this perspective, human adjustment can also be defined as the extent to which the individual accurately appraises his or her environment and is therefore able to cope with the demands of that environment.

The realist viewpoint can be contrasted with a *constructivist* perspective, which holds that the existence of an objective, external reality is wrong or, at the least, a weak and untestable premise. In the first instance, a *radical constructivist* perspective would be that the external world does not exist; that all that can and does exist is what we perceive and experience. In this sense, any one person's reality is uniquely situated in space and time, so that it is neither the same reality that that person "knew" yesterday nor the same reality that he or she will experience in the future. A somewhat weaker version of the constructivist perspective is that it is irrelevant whether an external reality exists because humans are fallible in their perception. As such, we will never know what "reality" is in any event, since our perceptions and experiences are always limited by the possible range of human experience, by our history and development experiences, and by our current state, which might either enhance or limit our possible set of experiences.

From a constructivist perspective, human adjustment is not defined by the *correspondence* between perception and the real world, but rather by the *coherence* or integrity of experience. Also from this perspective, language does not reflect our experience of the world, but it literally defines the world and how it can be perceived: "In a constructivist view, human beings are denied any direct access to an immediate reality beyond *language,* defined broadly as the entire repertory of symbolic utterances and actions afforded to use by our culture" (Neimeyer, 1995, p. 15, italics in original).

Realist and constructivist perspectives have often been contrasted, especially with regard to the epistemological underpinnings of each perspective and their attendant research methodologies (Mahoney, 1991). In particular, whereas a realist perspective is consistent with logical positivism and quantitative science, constructivism eschews a universal perspective on science and instead supports the use of qualitative methods in research, situated within the experience of individuals, who are in turn considered to be situated within a unique historical, cultural, and personal context (Guidano, 1984).

Cognitive therapy has been primarily associated with a realist perspective and epistemology. Evidence in support of this claim can be found in many writings. For example, cognitive therapists have discussed the individual as a "personal scientist" (Arnkoff, 1980; Mahoney, 1977) who seeks knowledge of the world and who can accurately perceive that reality or can have distorted perceptions. Some of the better-known techniques of cognitive therapy teach patients to recognize biases and distortions in perception and to have more realistic perceptions, so that the patient can solve problems in a "realistic" manner. In those instances in which it might not be clear whether the patient's perceptions are accurate or if there is simply not enough information, cognitive therapists may work with patients to gather "evidence" and discuss the implications of this new information. Cognitive therapists are comfortable with scales and measurement tools that have been developed through group and quantitative research; they also rely on diagnosis and research evidence, and they incorporate ideas related to evidence-based treatment (D. J. G. Dobson & Dobson, 2009) into case conceptualization and planning.

Other features of cognitive therapy are actually more consistent with constructivism. For example, cognitive therapists recognize that individuals have unique cultural, historical, and personal backgrounds, which shape the meanings that they assign to their experience: "The cognitive perspective posits . . . the dual existence of an objective reality and a personal, subjective, phenomenological reality" (Alford & Beck, 1997, p. 23). Put otherwise, the cognitive model posits that an individual's perceptions and appraisals are based in part on the objective nature of the event or experience, as might be experienced by anyone in that situation, and in part on the unique ways of knowing, language, and developmental experiences of the individual.

NATURE OF COGNITION

Within the overall cognitive model of human experience, distinctions are made among different types of cognition or thought. Various typologies or conceptualizations of cognition have arisen, but two are of particular relevance here: the *information processing model* and the *cognitive model of cognition.*

The information processing model of cognition is consistent with the idea that objective reality occurs and can be attended to, perceived, known, and stored in memory. A series of aspects of this cognitive system, including cognitive structures, content, processes, and products, have been distinguished (Ingram & Kendall, 1986; Kendall & Ingram, 1987). Each of these aspects is discussed next.

Cognitive structures represent the organization of long-term memories, which are held within the mind. These structures are composed of specific memories, situated at a specific place and time (sometimes referred to as *episodic* or *autobiographical* memory), as well as organized, linguistically based collections of memories (sometimes referred to as *semantic memory*). Semantic memory is the symbolic representation of the formal knowledge that is collected through experience and tends to be shared among people within a certain culture and during a historical period. By definition, however, autobiographical memory is unique and based on personal experience.

Both autobiographical and semantic memories are themselves structured. For example, they comprise different aspects of memory, including sensory aspects of knowledge and experience, but they also comprise linguistic, emotional, and even potentially bodily or behavioral aspects of knowledge. These memories are also hierarchically organized. For example, the autobiographical memory of "mother" will comprise a number of different events or interactions, not only with "my mother" but "mothers" in general, and even "not mother" (i.e., experiences that differentiate mother and mothering from different other types of experiences, such as "father" and "fathering"). Semantic memories can be formally hierarchical, for example, in the way that "living organisms" is a superordinate construct that encompasses animals, which in turn encompasses mammals, which in turn encompasses dogs (among other animals), which in turn encompasses specific breeds or types of dogs.

Cognitive structures not only represent a repository for the storage of memories but also guide the processing of new information. New information is more easily processed if there is an existing template or structure into which it can be placed. It appears that existing cognitive structures can actually bias attention to and processing of new information so that new information fits within them. Thus, once cognitive structures are established, they tend to be self-confirming or self-maintaining.

Cognitive content can be defined as the actual material that is held within cognitive structures or is the object of new information processing. Cognitive content is as variable as the range of human experience and includes words, images, memories, sensory experiences, fantasies, and emotions. There is a tendency in the cognitive literature to assume that cognitive content must be subject to verbal mediation—it must be named, or at least be nameable. However, this assumption is somewhat controversial, as some cognitive theorists would argue that even emotional memories are part of the content that humans can experience.

Cognitive processes include the various mechanisms through which information flows through the information processing system. They include the various sensory and attentional processes through which new experiences enter the system. They are known not to be literal copies of the external world but are potentially biased by the emotional state of the person who is attending to the environment and to preexisting structures. Once information comes into attention, various processes can either amplify the information (e.g., rehearsal of information) or reduce its salience (e.g., selective forgetting). Furthermore, if information is transferred into long-term memory, it can be either assimilated into existing memory structures, or if the experience is unique or bizarre, accommodation of the memory structures might be required to enable the memory to be retained.

Several cognitive processes are associated with memory for cognitive structures. Certain biases or heuristics might either enhance or diminish the opportunity to recall certain information. Some memories may depend on the actual state of the person, so that they are best recalled when the person tries to remember in a state that is similar to when the information was first put into memory. Some memories appear to be lost or repressed but are later accessible. It even appears that memories can be changed or manipulated to some extent.

The final aspect of the information processing model is *cognitive products*. These products are the specific cognitions that result from the dynamic interplay among cognitive structures, content, and processes. They can take the form of specific ideas or reactions to events, memories of events, or thoughts about or reflections on different experiences. Some cognitive products may occur very quickly or "automatically" if they involve well-used cognitive structures and processes, whereas others may only result from reflection and consideration. Cognitive products also exist in different forms, such as verbal utterances, images, or even emotional memories.

In contrast to the information processing model of cognition, as reflected in the constructs of structure, process, content, and product, the cognitive model of cognition was formulated specifically in the context of cognitive therapy. This model makes use of some of the same principles and processes as the information processing model, but the terminology is more specific, and the model is more attuned to the needs of a clinically useful way to consider these constructs. This model has been presented in graphical form in various sources (Alford & Beck, 1997; D. J. G. Dobson & Dobson, 2009) and is presented here in a more simplified fashion (see Figure 3.1).

According to the cognitive model, individuals possess cognitive structures, which are a composite of both formal (semantic) and personal (autobiographical or episodic) knowledge and experience. Various terms have been used to refer to these structures, but the most common are *beliefs* and *schemas.* Within the cognitive model, schemas are seen as both *reactive,* in that they respond to and incorporate new information, and *proactive,* in that they influence which types of situations a person might be willing to enter, the information that is attended to in different situations or contexts, and even the range of experiences an individual is able to have.

Because the schema construct is broad, there have been efforts to identify the possible content of schemas in various disorders. For example, in an early article about depression, A. T. Beck, Rush, Shaw, and Emery

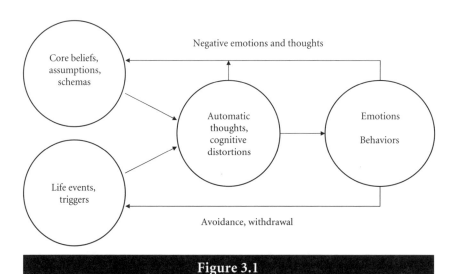

Figure 3.1

The cognitive–behavioral model of emotional distress. From *Evidence-Based Practice of Cognitive–Behavioral Therapy* (p. 44), by D. J. G. Dobson and K. S. Dobson, 2009, New York, NY: Guilford Press. Copyright 2009 by Guilford Press. Reprinted with permission.

(1979) discussed the *cognitive triad,* which consists of beliefs about the self, the world, and the future. They went on to specify typical or characteristic beliefs that a depressed person has in each of these three domains. Specifically, they suggested that depressed persons view themselves as "losers," that they are "helpless" in the world, and that the future is "hopeless." Over time, this model has been presented in various ways. Figure 3.2 depicts one version of an elaborated cognitive model of depression (Blackburn, James, & Flitcroft, 2006). As can be seen there, core beliefs and schemas interact dynamically with critical incidents or triggers to activate assumptions or behavior rules, as well as automatic thoughts, which then lead to the symptoms of depression.

Key schemas have been similarly identified in other disorders, such as the idea that the world is "dangerous" in anxiety disorders (A. T. Beck & Emery, 1985) or that other people are "hostile" for people with anger problems (A. T. Beck, 1999). Figure 3.3 presents a general cognitive model for panic disorder (D. M. Clark, 1986; Wells, 2006), Figure 3.4 represents a model for insomnia (Harvey, 2006), and Figure 3.5 is a model for anorexia nervosa (Lavender & Schmidt, 2006). Models either have been or are being developed for a wide range of other disorders and clinical problems (Tarrier, 2006).

It has been argued that schemas may also follow common patterns that cut across disorders. A. T. Beck, Epstein, Harrison, and Emery (1983) identified the two schema themes of sociotropy and autonomy to reflect this idea and developed the Sociotropy–Autonomy Scale (SAS) to measure these constructs. From this perspective, sociotropy reflects an interpersonal dependency and the personal belief that one needs interpersonal relations and support to function. Sociotropic persons are vulnerable to anxiety if their interpersonal relationships are threatened or to depression if these relationships are actually disrupted or broken. In contrast, autonomous persons tend to define themselves in terms of their individual achievements, accomplishments, and degree of independence or autonomy. Autonomous persons become anxious if their autonomy is threatened and depressed if they suffer a blow to their sense of achievement or accomplishment. These constructs are not specific to a particular disorder but cut across different emotional response patterns.

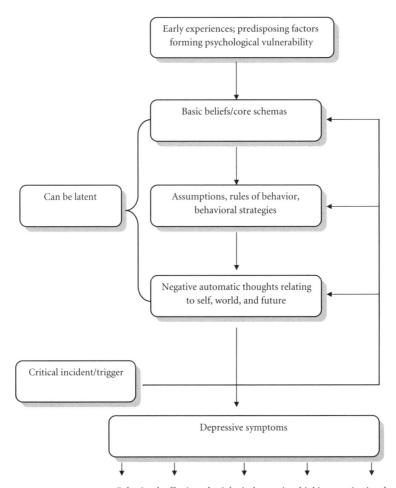

Figure 3.2

Cognitive model of depression. From *Case Formulation in Cognitive Behaviour Therapy: The Treatment of Challenging and Complex Cases* (p. 121), by N. Tarrier, 2006, New York, NY: Routledge. Copyright 2006 by Routledge. Reprinted with permission.

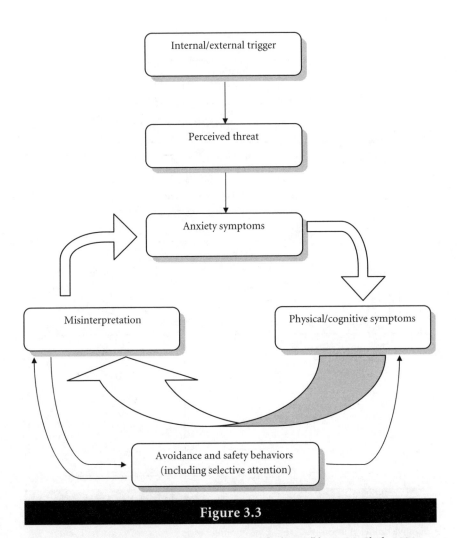

Figure 3.3

Cognitive model of panic. From "A Cognitive Model of Panic" by D. M. Clark, 1986, *Behavior Research and Therapy, 24,* p. 465 and *Case Formulation in Cognitive Behaviour Therapy: The Treatment of Challenging and Complex Cases* (p. 58), by N. Tarrier, 2006, New York, NY: Routledge. Copyright 2006 by Routledge. Adapted with permission.

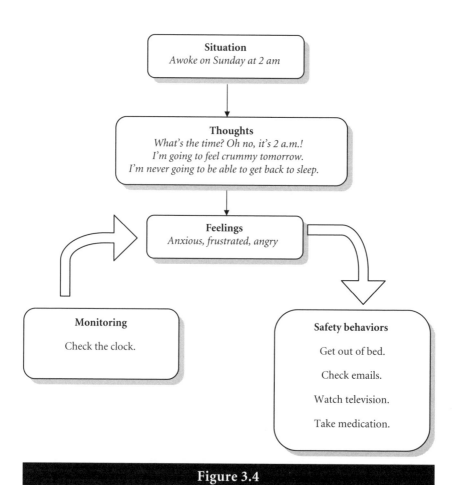

Figure 3.4

Cognitive model of insomnia. From *Case Formulation in Cognitive Behaviour Therapy: The Treatment of Challenging and Complex Cases* (p. 298), by N. Tarrier, 2006, New York, NY: Routledge. Copyright 2006 by Routledge. Adapted with permission.

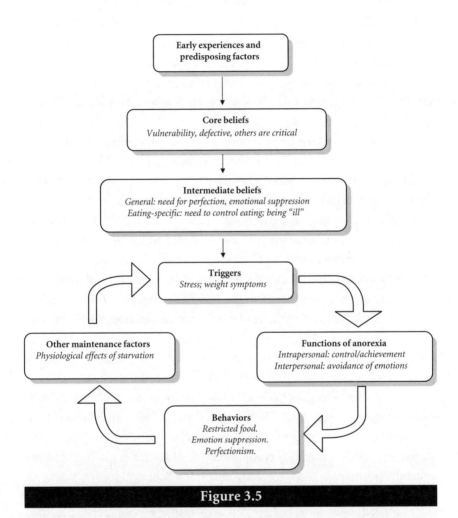

Figure 3.5

Cognitive model of anorexia nervosa. From *Case Formulation in Cognitive Behaviour Therapy: The Treatment of Challenging and Complex Cases* (p. 247), by N. Tarrier, 2006, New York, NY: Routledge. Copyright 2006 by Routledge. Adapted with permission.

Considerable research has been done to validate the SAS and to demonstrate its predictive validity. In general, the internal reliability and factor structure of the SAS have been substantiated (Bieling, Beck, & Brown, 2000, 2004; Ross & Clark, 1993). Research has also demonstrated that the dimension of Sociotropy interacts with interpersonal difficulties to predict depression, although the evidence in support of the construct of Autonomy has been somewhat more elusive to obtain (Bieling & Alden, 2001; Coyne & Whiffen, 1995; Raghavan, Le, & Berenbaum, 2002; Robins, Bagby, Rector, Lynch, & Kennedy, 1997).

A schema model has been developed in the context of personality disorders (Young, 1990; Young, Klosko, & Weishaar, 2003). This model lists 18 different negative or dysfunctional early maladaptive schemas (EMSs). These constructs are divided into five broad domains: abandonment/ instability, mistrust/abuse, emotional deprivation, defectiveness/shame, and social isolation/alienation. The specific EMSs are fairly closely related to different personality disorders in some instances, as for example in the area of "dependence/incompetence," which is similar to the idea of dependent personality disorder, as defined in the *Diagnostic and Statistical Manual of Mental Disorders* (4th ed.; American Psychiatric Association, 2000). In other instances, however, EMSs reflect broad and stable dimensions of functioning that potentially cut across disorders. For example, "failure" is likely a personal schema seen in a number of different disorders.

Young and colleagues (Young, 1990; Young et. al., 2003) have developed different scales to assess these schema dimensions. The Schema Questionnaire and its short form have been subjected to several psychometric studies, and despite the fairly complex nature of the scale, results have been generally positive (Lee, Taylor, & Dunn, 1999; Schmidt, Joiner, Young, & Telch, 1995). The short form of the Schema Questionnaire also has good internal reliability and factor structure (Welburn, Coristine, Dagg, Pontefract, & Jordan, 2002). The predictive value of these scales has yet to be fully evaluated, however.

Hypothetically, schemas develop naturally and spontaneously in everyone as major mechanisms that are used in making sense of the world and our lived experiences. Furthermore, every person has schemas in many different areas, some of which may be positive and some of which might be negative, depending on developmental experiences. One of the more difficult assumptions related to the schema model, however, is that schemas lie relatively dormant until primed or activated by a relevant situation or trigger. So, for example, a person who has a strong interpersonal dependency schema will function well and appear to be functionally independent, unless his or her interpersonal relationships are threatened, at which time negative thoughts, emotions, and behaviors might all be demonstrated. The assumption of "silent schemas" has been expressed as a diathesis–stress process, in that schemas represent a diathesis or vulnerability toward distress or dysfunctional behavior, but only when activated by a relevant stressor (Coyne & Whiffen, 1995; Robins & Block, 1989).

Once a schema is activated by a trigger or situation, the cognitive model holds that the information that the individual is experiencing is appraised. Appraisals can be benign or potentially positive, depending on the nature of the event and the corresponding schemas. Most of the focus in cognitive therapy, however, is on more insidious and negative appraisals. A. T. Beck et al. (1979) argued that in psychopathology, negative appraisals tend to be relatively reflexive and "automatic," as they reflect overlearned reactions to various types of situations. Although these appraisals or "automatic thoughts" are often made without conscious effort or deliberation, they can be brought to awareness and evaluated with appropriate training and skills.

The concept of automatic thoughts actually encompasses different aspects of the information processing model of cognition. The actual thoughts are the product of information processing, which includes attention to the trigger or stimulus situation, thoughts about the situation (e.g., rumination, distorted appraisals), appraisals of the meaning of the situation as mediated by the schemas, and the production of a cognitive product, which is the thought itself. Cognitive theorists have elucidated a variety of possible ways in which situations can be misperceived or distorted to yield negative outcomes (A. T. Beck et al., 1979; J. S. Beck, 1995). Patients use these cognitive distortions selectively, in ways that help to maintain the integrity and stability of schemas, even sometimes at the risk of emotional health.

As noted previously, appraisal of an event is not sufficient for it to cause distress, even if it activates a relevant schema. For example, a person with a failure schema might be passed over for a promotion at her place of work. In some instances, such an event might activate the sense of failure and inadequacy. However, other circumstances might interfere with such an interpretation. For example, her supervisor might argue that since she was not in the workplace as long as another colleague, union rules required that the other person receive primary consideration. It is thus only when the event triggers a schema *and* the meaning attached to the situation is negative (e.g., "I was passed over for the promotion *because* my supervisor knows I can't do the job; I am stuck in this lower level position forever") that the consequences are likely to be negative. Thus, the evidence and facts of the situation, as well as their meaning, are part of the process that generates negative automatic thoughts.

Once a schema has been activated and a negative automatic thought has been generated, the cognitive model further stipulates that consequences will follow. Specifically, negative emotions and behaviors are expected, consistent with the nature of the cognitive appraisals. For example, if an appraisal of a pending event is that it is unpredictable or uncontrollable, then most likely the emotional consequence of this appraisal will be fear or anxiety, and the behavioral outcome will be avoidance. This process has been labeled *cognitive specificity* (D. A. Clark, Beck, & Alford, 1999; D. A. Clark, Beck, & Stewart, 1990), and considerable evidence supports the idea that fairly defined forms of cognition are associated with distinct emotional patterns and behavioral outcomes.

Although most descriptions of the cognitive model of appraisal end with the emotional or behavioral outcome, these outcomes in turn have feedback implications. Thus, if a person becomes anxious and aroused, other anxiety-related thoughts become more likely, as the relevant schema has been activated and "primed" to influence the appraisal of other novel situations. Also, behaviors themselves have consequences. First, most people notice and appraise their own actions. A socially anxious person who avoids certain social settings, for example, may observe that avoidance and use that behavior as further evidence of his or her social ineptitude or social undesirability. Furthermore, by taking certain actions, an individual makes certain beliefs more likely. For example, a socially avoidant person is unlikely to have a pleasant social experience and learn that he or she is not as socially awkward or undesirable as may be believed; thus, avoidance allows certain negative schemas to be maintained or even strengthened.

COGNITION, EMOTION, BEHAVIOR, AND THE SOCIAL ENVIRONMENT

Cognitive models posit a complex set of interactions among cognition, emotion, behavior, and the social environment. They recognize that schemas are developed in a social context, and while schemas are developmentally based, they begin to exert an ongoing influence once they are established. In this regard, they tend to become more stable over time, especially as the individual starts to identify with these schemas and limits his or her range of experiences to be consistent with these self-schemas. It is also probable that over time, as children grow to become adults, they engineer their social environments to be consistent with their self-schemas and to select people to interact with who support these perceptions.

Cognitive models have been criticized for giving "primacy" to cognitive processes (Coyne & Gotlib, 1983) and relegating emotions and behaviors to consideration as epiphenomenal experience. In contrast, Zajonc (1980) argued that certain experiences are sensory or emotional in nature and do not require cognitive processing. There is now considerable research in the domain of "effortful" and "automatic" information processing (Hartlage, Alloy, Vasquez, & Dykman, 1993). Furthermore, recent descriptions of cognitive therapy tend to recognize the reciprocal influences of cognition, emotion, behavior, and the environment more than did earlier descriptions, which tended to be somewhat more linear. However, cognitive mediation of situations and events is a principal assumption of the cognitive model of psychopathology (K. S. Dobson & Dozois, 2010), and this assumption is reflected in the key interventions of cognitive therapy. Thus, although cognitive therapists will at times use more behavioral or directly emotive therapy techniques, the majority of the methods rely on cognitive mediation, reinterpretation, or both mediation and reinterpretation for their effect.

THE STABILITY HYPOTHESIS AND PSYCHOTHERAPY

The cognitive model proposes that schemas are based on developmental experiences, which can include early interactions with parents, early exposure to different types of living environments, and different social interactions. Schemas are also based on messages that are received from the world at large, such as television, radio, and print media. As children grow and develop their own social circles, these relationships also exert an influence on schema development and maintenance. In theory, a newborn can develop a wide range of possible schemas, and he or she is capable of developing either a generally positive or negative set of schemas, depending on subsequent social and environmental interactions. However, the model suggests that as schemas develop, they tend to become more fixed, to moderate the reaction to the social environment, and even to direct the nature of the way that the growing child interacts with the world. Although there is no particular age or developmental stage at which schemas become immutable, the general assumption is that the more rigid, absolute, and inflexible schemas cause problems.

If schemas are in some cases problematic, why do they develop? There are two general processes by which children develop schemas that become problems for them later in life. One is that the parents are themselves disturbed in some way, and they inadvertently engage in behaviors that cause schema problems in their children. For example, a mother who is depressed may have significant difficulty in affect regulation, and as a result she may have problems bonding emotionally with her child (Garber & Martin, 2002). Thus, despite her best intentions and even though she may do the best she can, she might still engender difficulties in her child's ability to form such relationships. Or a parent who from time to time becomes aggressive and hurts the child may teach the child that he or she is "unlovable," or at least is only lovable when the parent's mood is stable. These early experiences can leave cognitive scars in the child, which are carried forward in the form of cognitive schemas and interpersonal behavior patterns.

The second possibility is that whereas the bases of schemas develop primarily in childhood, when the child is dependent on others for sustenance and care, schemas survive into adulthood, when the person is now responsible for his or her own care. Cognitive and behavioral patterns that were functional in childhood may well become dysfunctional in adulthood. For example, imagine a child who has an emotionally needy parent, who often is overinvolved in the child's development. In such a case, the child may learn to be functionally dependent on the parent, and this dependency will be mutually reinforcing. However, the child may learn through this process that he or she is incompetent and as an adult may struggle with making independent decisions or living an autonomous and adult life. Indeed, a general notion is that schemas typically make sense or are functional when they develop but they may persist past their point of optimal utility.

4

The Therapy Process

If schemas, once established, are relatively permanent and tend to resist change, how does change happen during the process of psychotherapy? This issue has been a matter of considerable discussion among those interested in cognitive therapy. It has been argued that cognitive therapy has aspects of coping/problem solving and of schema change (Arnkoff, 1986). From a coping skills/problem-solving perspective, patients in cognitive therapy learn a set of tools with which they can approach their problems after treatment. Most patients come to treatment with a set of problems, and an initial stage of cognitive therapy is helping patients to name, differentiate, and evaluate the extent of these problems. The cognitive therapist and patient will work to solve these problems or to minimize their negative effects. A substantial amount of time in cognitive therapy is spent in teaching new skills that can be used to undermine existing problems. As described below, these types of skills are particularly emphasized when the patient's problems are seen to be "realistic," that is, to have considerable basis in the social environment in which the patient lives.

However, the model also notes that core schemas form part of the basis of the development of problems. As such, schema change can undermine problems, or at least the perception that a current social situation is problematic. Indeed, a number of interventions in cognitive therapy promote schema change. These interventions are predicated on the belief that schemas evolve naturally over time and that new experiences are assimilated into an existing schema where possible, or that they force change in the schemas if they cannot be assimilated. Thus, as the patient has new and more positive interactions with the therapist and others over the course of therapy, it is hoped that he or she will assimilate the ideas of appropriate and healthy views of the self and social interactions into his or her self-schemas. During the course of therapy the therapist and patient may together design experiences that test the very foundations of problematic schemas. In some cases the patient may have experiences that cannot be assimilated into existing schemas but that require the schema to change to accommodate them. For example, a man whose core identity is one of being socially undesirable may learn the skills to modify his ways of thinking and behaving over time and with coaching and training might find a meaningful, caring relationship. The development of this relationship may severely test the extent of the existing undesirable self-schema and might require its modification, elimination, or replacement.

Cognitive therapy is a complex form of psychotherapy. It rests on a particular patient–therapist relationship, and this relationship is considered to be a necessary but not sufficient aspect of the treatment. The techniques of cognitive therapy include aspects of problem identification and problem solving, cognitive and behavioral skills training, and schema identification and modification. Which specific techniques are used with which patient, in what order, and with what outcomes are predicated on an individualized case assessment and conceptualization. Achieving the ability to form a therapeutic relationship, to assess and conceptualize diverse cases, to select and to apply a broad range of possible techniques takes time, training, supervision, and practice (D. J. G. Dobson & Dobson, 2009).

PRINCIPLES OF COGNITIVE THERAPY

Cognitive therapy rests on certain principles or assumptions. This chapter presents these principles, which are essential elements of competent cognitive therapy (see Exhibit 4.1). However, not all of the principles of cognitive therapy will necessarily be observed in every case. Thus, while cognitive therapists are trained in all of the principles, they use clinical judgment in each case in determining how to maximize the treatment process and which specific skills or principles to employ to attain treatment outcomes. As described in more detail in Chapter 5, cognitive therapists also develop a case conceptualization for each patient, which figures largely in the clinical decisions the therapist makes with respect to which principles are emphasized or given less weight.

Focus on Current Adaptation and Present Problems

Cognitive therapy represents a pragmatic philosophy toward psychotherapy. Patients seek the services of a psychotherapist when they have problems to solve. More to the point, they come for such services when their own efforts to solve these problems have failed. In the first instance, then, cognitive therapy is a system for solving problems (D. J. G. Dobson & Dobson, 2009).

Problem solving can be described as a process that involves a series of interactive steps. The steps include identifying and naming the problem, generating alternative ways to solve the problem, choosing the most likely

---

Exhibit 4.1   Principles of Cognitive Therapy

- Focus on current adaptation and present problems
- Time-limited treatment
- Structured therapy
- Key role of activity and homework
- Focus on the therapeutic relationship
- Collaborative empiricism
- Psychoeducation
- Technical eclecticism
- Treatment as prevention

---

successful strategy, implementing the chosen strategy, assessing the out-come(s) of the strategy, and then either stopping the process (if the strat-egy is successful) or else cycling back to the beginning to reconsider the problem and choose a new strategy (D'Zurilla & Nezu, 2007). Problem solving also rests on a generally positive attitude toward problems. Specif-ically, one needs to believe that the problem can be solved and that the effort is worthwhile. This "problem-solving orientation" (Nezu, Nezu, & Lombardo, 2004) sometimes needs to be cultivated; although patients may wish or hope that their problems will remit, they are sometimes not com-mitted fully to the course of action that might be recommended or required for the desired outcome.

Even if a patient comes to treatment with a strong and positive orienta-tion toward solving a problem, it is almost certainly the case that he or she has failed in his or her own efforts to do so. This failure can be demoralizing, and some time to address this sense of failure and helplessness in treatment may be required before new efforts can be attempted. In some cases, a type of motivational interviewing is needed to encourage patients to see the potential advantages of making an effort. However, failure can also indi-cate a skills deficit or a lack of ability on the part of the patient to approach the problem effectively. In such cases, therapy may need to include educa-tion or training in potential strategies that can then be utilized. In other cases, patients may have a desire to change and even a sense of how to accomplish change, but they may face external pressures or challenges that preclude the use of the intended plan. The external forces may include prag-matic problems such as a lack of funds or physical impairment or social impediments such as unsupportive families or partners. In such cases, these impediments may need to be addressed before the main change process can be approached.

In ideal circumstances, the patient comes to therapy with a specific list of problems, and the therapist can quickly identify strategies that the patient has not previously tried, one of which turns out to be effective. Unfortunately, this simplistic process rarely occurs. In some cases, the patient presents with a number of severe, chronic, or severe and chronic problems. Indeed, in many cases patients wait until the problem is too severe to tolerate or until several attempts to address the problem have failed before they seek help. Sometimes the delay in seeking help exacerbates the problem.

One of the first tasks a cognitive therapist will undertake is to list the presenting problems. The list is developed into a specific set of potential treatment targets. With the patient, the therapist prioritizes the problems from the most to the least significant. The therapist may take some time to understand the patient's perception of the problem list, as this is one of the first opportunities to understand the patient's worldview and sense of agency. The development of the problem list also provides the first opportunity for the therapist to communicate to the patient a desire to hear about concerns and problems and to demonstrate a willingness to work with the patient on these issues.

Sometimes the patient presents a set of problems that do not fit into a cognitive therapy formulation. For example, one patient may want to focus on understanding her problematical childhood. Another may seem fixated on blaming others for his unsatisfactory job performance or life situation. In such cases, the cognitive therapist will attempt to reorient the patient to problems that can be addressed with cognitive therapy methods. So, for example, the patient with the problematic childhood will be asked about the effect of her childhood on her current relationships and view of herself. The angry and blaming patient will be asked what role he has in his own problems, since he can control only his own behavior. Such questions help to show the patient that the problem is heard but focus the patient on current problems.

The therapist and the patient may have a difference of opinion about problem priorities. For example, a patient may want to talk about her childhood, whereas the therapist believes that her current unemployment is more urgent. In such cases, the cognitive therapist will typically express this difference of viewpoint and then take the patient's direction. This response is made in the belief that if the more important problem is not addressed, it will still be present when the therapist and patient finally get to it. Furthermore, cognitive therapists believe that responsiveness to the patient's perceived needs will build therapeutic rapport. Exceptions to this general rule can be made if the patient or someone in his or her life might be placed at risk in the event that an issue is not attended to or there is a legal or ethical imperative requiring priority attention. In such cases, the patient should be provided with the rationale for the therapist's decisions and actions so that even if the patient does not concur with the decision, he or she at least understands the therapist's actions.

Finally, in some instances it might not be possible to agree on treatment goals. For example, agreement may be impossible if the therapist determines that there are safety issues but the patient is unwilling to address them. In such instances, it is appropriate for the therapist and patient to agree to disagree. The most ethical course of action may well be to refer the patient to another therapist.

A problem-focused therapy implies a concomitant responsibility to assess the patient's problems over time. Therefore, cognitive therapists often make use of standardized tests of psychological maladjustment to monitor reduction in symptoms. Cognitive therapists also rely on self-reported behaviors, activity charts, self-monitoring forms, global ratings of change, and other reported change indices to ensure that the problems being treated are in fact responding to the interventions. In some cases, goal attainment scaling (Kiresuk, Stelmachers, & Schultz, 1982) can also be profitably used to determine progress in achieving goals.

Time-Limited Treatment

Because cognitive therapy is focused on the resolution of specific problems and issues, it is by definition a time-limited treatment. The cognitive therapist is trying to "put himself or herself out of business" as quickly as possible with each patient. Protocols exist for a number of disorders, and the protocols often limit the number of recommended sessions. Even when a specific recommendation does not exist regarding the length of treatment, there is a sense that treatment should be focused and goal-oriented. These ideas can be communicated to the patient in the following ways: predictions by the therapist about the needed length of therapy, regular reviews of treatment progress, conscious efforts to transfer learning to the patient so that he or she can manage on his or her own, statements by the therapist about the pending end of treatment, and reviews of treatment process and outcomes. Even in cases where the problems are more amorphous, the therapist will discuss with the patient at intervals how treatment is going, what goal or goals are being served, and how much longer treatment might last.

Structured Therapy

Although the amount of structure in cognitive therapy can be over-emphasized, as the approach is flexible in terms of how it is conducted, cognitive therapy does tend to be more structured than other forms of psychotherapy. This structure can be observed both within the context of any given session and across treatment sessions.

Intrasession Structure

Three distinct phases can be observed within each session of cognitive therapy. These phases can be conceptualized as a preparation phase, the "work," and a completion phase. In the preparation phase, the therapist and patient greet each other and may engage in some small talk as they get settled. If the patient has completed any questionnaires or measures between sessions, the therapist will review them and might summarize their results. The therapist will inquire about events since the previous session and ascertain whether anything extraordinary has occurred that might require attention in the current session. If there has been a particular focus of therapy, there will often be a quick check-in about that issue. For example, if the focus has been on worry, the therapist might ask how much of a problem worry has been in the interval since the prior session. There might also be a "mood check" in the form of a rating from 0 to 100 if the focus of treatment has been on the reduction of a particular negative emotion.

The cognitive therapist will always inquire whether the patient was able to complete any assignment that was set during the previous session. If so, the results of the assignment will be quickly ascertained. If the homework was not attempted or if the patient had a significant problem with its completion, time will be set aside to determine what that problem was and how the assignment might be reattempted. Toward the end of the preparatory phase, the therapist will ask the patient whether he or she wants to focus on any particular issues in the current session. The therapist may add a topic if there is a particular technique or method that he or she wants to introduce or to develop. Together, the therapist and patient consider the range of items they want to include on a final agenda, prioritize them to ensure that the most important topics are addressed first and in the most detail, and perhaps assign time limits to some or all of the items to ensure that all the issues are adequately discussed. The entire preparatory phase takes at most 10 minutes, but more typically only about 5 minutes once the important topics have been established and the therapist and patient are meeting regularly.

After the agenda has been set, the topics are addressed. This work phase of therapy is the most diverse in form, as the nature of what is discussed and the methods that are used will vary dramatically across patients, problems, and phases of therapy. In general, this is the phase of the session wherein the therapist and patient together name and solve the patient's problems by using a range of interventions. As described more fully below, at the conclusion of a topic discussion, an assignment or homework is often developed as a way to enact a concrete change in the patient's life. The therapist keeps general track of the time and ensures that all of the important topics receive the attention they need in the session.

After each topic on the agenda has been discussed, the therapist will usually note that the therapy session is coming to an end. He or she will often invite the patient to summarize the session or to identify what he or she considers the most important things discussed. For example, the therapist might ask, "What are the most important things that you will take away from today's appointment?" The response will help the therapist learn what the patient has attended to and will allow for either correction with regard to certain issues or a focus on other issues that the therapist wants to bring to the patient's attention.

The ending part of the session also involves a review of the homework assignments that were developed over the course of the therapy session. The review may entail writing all of the homework down on an agenda form or in a notebook. It might also involve an adjustment of the homework, since there may be too little homework or too much to reasonably accomplish before the next session. The therapist often will ask for overall feedback about the session to ensure that the patient feels that his or her concerns were addressed and that the relationship is an effective one. The therapist might comment about the progress of therapy or briefly discuss some particularly successful or difficult aspects of the session. Finally, the date and time of the next session are set, payment is made (if relevant), and the patient leaves.

Intersession Structure

Just as there is a structure within sessions, there is often a structure to cognitive therapy across sessions. There may be a movement from a behavioral focus and a restoration of adaptive functioning to a focus on negative automatic thoughts and potential cognitive distortions and eventually to an examination and possible modification of underlying beliefs and schemas. The exact content of the work will vary from case to case, as different general conceptualizations guide the treatment of different disorders for different patients. Also, cognitive therapists are willing to backtrack and address an issue that was dealt with earlier in the course of therapy if it resurfaces or requires further attention.

Although there is considerable structure to the practice of cognitive therapy, the above ideas are general guideposts rather than rigid rules. Cognitive therapy is a flexible system of treatment, and therapists will sometimes modify the structure to respond to clinical exigencies. For example, if the patient divulges suicidal intent halfway through a session, the therapist will often postpone the work that is under way while a suicide assessment and intervention are conducted. A cognitive therapist might consciously set a single topic for a session's agenda, if that topic is of critical importance at a given stage of therapy, although cognitive therapy sessions typically involve two to four topics in the work phase. If a patient is particularly distraught or having difficulties with concentration, the therapist might purposely shorten the session with the knowledge that although less will be covered, what is covered is likely to be remembered and acted upon.

Key Roles of Activity and Homework

As discussed in Chapter 3, cognitive therapy is one of the cognitive–behavioral therapies. In this context, it should not be a surprise to learn that cognitive therapists assess and promote both cognitive and behavioral change in the service of overall better adaptation and functioning. Indeed, consistent with the realist aspect of the cognitive model, cognitive therapists are conscious of the need to translate whatever is discussed in the therapy session into concrete action. One could even argue that what goes on *between* therapy sessions could be considered more important that what goes on *within* each session.

Because of the perceived importance of real-world change in cognitive therapy, cognitive therapists often use homework activities. Such homework is highly variable in its content, as it varies from case to case, within cases over time, and across different problems. In some cases, homework is used to gather new information about how the patient functions in his or her social environment. In others, it might be used to gather evidence to assess the validity of certain negative thoughts. Homework might serve to elicit new thoughts, which can then be examined and discussed in the coming treatment sessions. The therapist and patient may agree to homework that promotes schema change.

The idea of homework carries some unfortunate connotations. The first is that of school and that homework in cognitive therapy is merely an educational activity. Such an inference is not correct, since homework in cognitive therapy could be just as easily called a task, a mission, a challenge, an experiment, or an assignment. Indeed, if school has a negative association for the patient, the word *homework* might best be avoided.

The second possible connotation is that homework is simply educative. Again, this inference is erroneous. Homework is often educative, but it can also be investigative, confrontational, or experiential. In addition, homework can be directed toward thoughts or behavioral change. It can also be directed to changes in relationships, emotional experiences, and even physiology (e.g., diet changes, medication changes). The term is in some ways a catchall for any translation of therapy discussion into a concrete change in the way that the patient relates to his or her world.

Homework is *always* used in good cognitive therapy (Kazantzis & Deane, 1999; Kazantzis, Deane, Ronan, & L'Abate, 2005). The cognitive therapist is constantly on the lookout for methods to create lasting change in the patient's problems and will stay mindful of possible homework assignments. As the focus of a therapy session moves from one area to another, the therapist will summarize what has been discussed (or have the patient provide a summary) and will ask about a possible homework assignment. Early in the course of therapy, the therapist may propose assignments, but as therapy progresses and the patient learns about assignments, the therapist will often transfer the task of setting assignments to the patient. Ideally, both the therapist and patient will concur about the importance of any given assignment, and both will leave the therapy session with a clear idea of what the homework is, when it will be conducted, and what the potential outcomes are.

A Focus on the Therapeutic Relationship

Cognitive therapists believe that a positive therapeutic relationship is necessary but not a sufficient criterion for effective psychotherapy. They are mindful of Rogerian principles and practices, or the so-called nonspecific variables of psychotherapy (Craighead, Sheets, Bjornsson, & Amarson, 2005). They also attend to the literature on therapist characteristics and styles that promote therapeutic change (Castonguay & Beutler, 2006), as well as to methods to promote an effective therapeutic alliance (Safran, 1998; Safran & Muran, 2000). Cognitive therapists also recognize and attend to "therapy ruptures" (J. S. Beck, 1995), problems in the therapeutic alliance, and resistance in cognitive therapy (Leahy, 2001). They also attend to both the patient's negative affective experiences with and toward the therapist, and the therapist's negative thoughts and feelings toward the patient. Such processes and reactions can inhibit treatment, and although they ideally do not become the focus of the therapy, they need to be monitored and, if necessary, overcome so that the focus of therapy can remain on the patient's problems.

Several aspects of the therapeutic relationship are promoted in cognitive therapy. The therapist and patient hopefully begin therapy with a general attitude of respect toward each other. Patients typically come to therapy with the idea that they are interacting with an expert and are often deferential toward the therapist. Hopefully, the therapist reciprocates this attitude and respects patients' efforts to struggle with life's problems and their willingness to seek assistance. The cognitive therapist tries to evaluate the patient's own coping skills and competencies and will work with existing skills while trying to strengthen these aptitudes during course of therapy. The patient is considered the expert in his or her own life, and cognitive therapists respect this unique position.

Cognitive therapists are encouraged to care about their patients and to demonstrate empathy. In this regard, cognitive therapists do not differ from therapists in other schools of psychotherapy, since these characteristics are viewed as facilitating a positive relationship (Castonguay & Beutler, 2006). They try to have open and direct communication with their patients to maximize the effective and reciprocal transmission of ideas, feelings, and concerns. As is true of other schools of therapy, cognitive therapists are expected to behave in an ethical manner toward their patients and not to exploit them for financial or personal gain.

Collaborative Empiricism

One idea that cognitive therapy has contributed to the area of positive therapeutic relationships is collaborative empiricism. This term reflects two intersecting notions. The first is that the therapist and patient work together as a team to identify problems, areas of needed change, and the optimal ways to effect change in the patient's life. As noted earlier, the therapist recognizes and respects the patient's competencies and skills, even while the patient comes to the therapist for expert advice and guidance in solving problems. The idea of a partnership evolves during the course of therapy. Often, in the early stages, the therapist is dominant and will provide ideas to the patient about new ways to think about or approach his or her problems. These proposals are always provided as suggestions and are discussed and approved by the patient before being considered as homework. As problems are overcome and the patient learns the methods of cognitive therapy, increasing control is given to him or her. Thus, the patient may suggest topics for discussion in a given session and will be encouraged by the therapist to set the homework himself or herself, with the therapist's responses, questions, and support. Cognitive therapy is not provided *to* patients but is conducted *with* patients as active partners.

The second aspect of the concept of collaborative empiricism relates to the notions of evidence and objectivism. The cognitive model recognizes that all humans misperceive events in the world, as our schemas to some extent color or shade what we see and how we view events. Cognitive therapists recognize that if therapy is limited to talking about events or experience, any discussion might be predicated on erroneous perceptions or ideas. Thus, the therapist encourages the patient through discussion and homework to evaluate the facts of the matter and to separate perception from evidence as much as possible. If the evidence related to a particular key cognition is insufficient, the homework assignment may be no more than to ascertain the objective "truth" as much as possible. Once the evidence is clear, it can be evaluated independently of the meaning attached to it or of the emotional responses engendered by that meaning.

A challenging situation in cognitive therapy arises when the patient asks for the advice or opinion of the therapist. In general, cognitive therapists work with patients to generate strategies that will work in the patient's life, and the patient is the best judge of outcomes. Cognitive therapists are reluctant to give the patient the "correct" or "best" answer, since such an answer rarely exists. Furthermore, because the therapist does not have to live out the consequences of decisions that are made in treatment, it is more ethical for the patient to determine the course of his or her own life. Thus, the cognitive therapist often asks the patient what he or she thinks (which also is an assessment of the patient's coping abilities and thoughts about the situation). In some instances, the answer to this question reveals a skills deficit, which might be addressed through reading or instruction and practice. In other cases, the answer reveals a negative thought, which can become the focus of an intervention. If the patient persists with appeals for the therapist's ideas, the therapist might inquire what others would do in a similar situation. Sometimes this question can lead to homework in which the patient canvasses other people to get some ideas. If pushed further, the therapist might offer one or more suggestions, and the therapist and patient can discuss the various options and select one that would work for the patient.

The patient may persist in asking the therapist's opinion or advice. The cognitive therapist will want to assess the meaning that the patient attaches to this advice. If the patient's belief is that "the therapist always knows best," this assumption would likely be addressed as absolutistic and erroneous, and the therapist might offer examples of how he or she does not always know best before giving a suggestion. When the belief is that "if the therapist cares about me, he will tell me what he would do," the therapist can offer other evidence that supports his or her caring and concern and then choose whether to provide the suggestion. If the patient's motive is to tell the therapist how his or her idea won't work or to challenge the therapist, providing an answer is likely to be unhelpful to the patient and possibly destructive to the therapy relationship. In such cases, the therapist might refuse to provide a suggestion.

Psychoeducation

Cognitive therapists want to work with their patients and help them solve their problems. Unfortunately, different people obtain more or less education, training, and support as they grow up, so they have more or less information with which to approach life. In cases in which people clearly do not have the necessary information to address problems, the cognitive therapist may enlist the support of other experts and sources of information or provide education himself or herself. For example, if a couple's concern is about the management of shared finances, the therapist might recommend a consultation with a financial planner or accountant. If the patient has a legal problem, referral to a lawyer might be the most effective and efficient strategy. A resourceful therapist will keep a list of current community agencies and services that can be recruited into therapy, when appropriate.

In some cases, education is clearly relevant to the problems that the patient brings into therapy, and the use of therapy time to provide information or instruction is likely to be beneficial. The therapist might use self-help books, CDs, DVDs, or other materials as an aid to therapy. The list of self-help books and patient manuals in the area of cognitive therapy is growing, and the therapist will likely want to keep some materials in the major problem areas that he or she works with on the bookshelf. Additional resources can be found online (see http://www.academyofct.org, click "Consumers").

Even when external materials or resources are not involved in cognitive therapy, the therapist will typically educate the patient about the work that is being conducted. Thus, the therapist will share the overall model with the patient early in the course of therapy to see whether the patient accepts the model and to show its relevance to the case. The cognitive therapist frequently will explain the rationale for the specific techniques that are selected and applied over the course of therapy. In general, the therapist wants to ensure that the patient has a good understanding of all the techniques and knows how to use them effectively and adaptively so that they can be reused, even after treatment has ended. In principle (although not in practice), the patient should be sufficiently conversant with the techniques so that he or she could actually treat another person.

Technical Eclecticism

One of the striking features of cognitive therapy is that a wide range of specific techniques, including the hallmark cognitive therapy techniques, are incorporated (Leahy, 2003; McMullin, 2000; W. T. O'Donohue & Fisher, 2009). The interventions chosen in cognitive therapy might just as easily emphasize behavioral assessment or change, emotional assessment or change, or assessment or change of physiological parameters (e.g., diet, exercise, sleep). A creative therapist is not restricted in the use of techniques as long as the methods can be framed within the overall cognitive case conceptualization and are structured to promote change in the patient's problem areas.

The technical eclecticism that is part of cognitive therapy presents something of a conundrum for therapists in training. Most often, trainees want to know what to do and when to do it. They often prefer a prescriptive manual to an open system of therapy, as a manual provides structure and support for their work. Manuals have their place. They are particularly useful when patients with similar concerns are being treated or when the nature of the problem is reasonably similar from case to case, even if the content of therapy varies. However, the individual application of cognitive therapy rests more on case conceptualization and understanding of the cognitive model. Knowledge of the model permits the therapist to create or adapt interventions as needed.

Treatment as Prevention

A corollary of some of the above principles is that cognitive therapists try not only to treat the present problems but also to reduce the likelihood of their recurrence as well as to develop skill sets in their patients to respond to any such recurrence. Thus, the use of a case formulation that rests on the cognitive model provides a certain structure for understanding each case, and this formulation can be communicated to the patient for reuse when necessary after therapy has ended. Moreover, since the treatment addresses underlying schemas, which represent vulnerability or risk factors for dysfunction, successful cognitive therapy should reduce the likelihood of future problems.

Evidence for the prophylactic nature of cognitive therapy has been demonstrated for a number of disorders (Antony, Ledley, & Heimberg, 2005). Debate continues about whether treatment effects are due to changes in core schemas and resulting reduction in risk or to improved coping methods and skills (DeRubeis et al., 1990). In any event, the reduced relapse rates seen after successful cognitive therapy, especially compared with pharmacotherapy, certainly imply that risk is being reduced with cognitive therapy.

THE PRACTICE OF COGNITIVE THERAPY: BEGINNING STEPS

Cognitive therapy is a systematic and purposeful psychotherapy that seeks to help the patient make meaningful life changes. Such changes include the reduction of symptoms or the elimination of a particular diagnosis, reduction of distress, improvements in daily living, an enhanced ability to cope with future stressors, and changes in core schemas to reduce the risk of future problems. As noted in previous chapters, a number of specific cognitive models and interventions have been developed for different diagnostic problems, and more generic concepts and techniques are commonly used as well. Given the range of possible therapist activities, how does the cognitive therapist determine which particular interventions to use with a particular patient?

Part of the answer to this question, of course, lies in the performance of an adequate intake assessment. This chapter presents the general beginning steps that a cognitive therapist would use with a person who has presented as a potential patient. In many practices, a moderately structured assessment is conducted before a decision is made to proceed with therapy. The assessment allows the therapist to consider whether the patient's problems can be well conceptualized and treated from a cognitive therapy model, the patient is sufficiently motivated to initiate therapy at the present time, any mitigating circumstances or disorders might need to be treated prior to cognitive therapy (e.g., substance abuse, domestic violence, physical or economic hardship), or whether any other consideration might lead the therapist to refer the patient for another type of treatment. From the patient's perspective, a sense of trust and confidence in the therapist, a willingness to work and invest effort in treatment, and a sense that the therapy is appropriate for him or her are important.

Intake Assessment

The intake assessment process usually involves a series of steps: the potential use of questionnaires or other test instruments, an intake interview, the development of a preliminary case conceptualization, a discussion with the patient about the appropriateness of the approach for him or her, a discussion of treatment goals, and the development of a preliminary contract for therapy.

Therapists and therapy practices vary in their use of assessment instruments. In some private practice settings the case documentation may consist of an information sheet about each patient (e.g., contact information, billing information, next of kin), notes from interviews and therapy sessions, and little else. In some group practices more formal documentation may include basic information about each patient, a standard intake questionnaire related to the presenting problem and any other health concerns the patient may have, consent forms for release of information and for assessment or therapy, and case notes. In hospital or university clinic settings, where databases are more typically used, the above information is commonly obtained from each patient, and this information may be supplemented by standard questionnaires that are used to document the initial state of the patient and treatment progress.

A wide range of questionnaires can be used in intake assessment. Which questionnaire or set of questionnaires will be employed is often a matter of therapist preference, but it may also depend on the type of practice setting. For example, an outpatient clinical service that offers general mental health treatment will likely incorporate assessment of anxiety or depression in an instrument battery, since these problems often present in such a setting.

Almost all therapists use the clinical interview as part of the intake assessment process. The clinical interview is a highly flexible tool for obtaining information from patients. The interview can focus on specific issues or problems and therefore take little time to conduct, or it can be comprehensive and take hours to complete. It can be unstructured and flexible to the needs of the patient or highly structured to obtain standardized and wide-ranging information. The interview can serve as a standalone assessment process, or it can be a prelude to psychotherapy. Which form of interview process is the most appropriate for a given setting and patient is a judgment best made by the clinician.

In the context of cognitive therapy, certain domains of information are almost always obtained (D. J. G. Dobson & Dobson, 2009). They include the presenting problem or problems, since a major focus of the treatment will be their reduction or elimination. A problem list can include symptoms, diagnoses, emotional states, cognitive or psychological problems, interpersonal disputes or dysfunction, substance use problems, health concerns, financial worries, legal difficulties, school or occupational difficulties, leisure concerns, problems of other people such as children or intimate partners, problems of daily living such as housing or transportation, problems with mental health treatment, or any combination of the these concerns.

The assessment during the intake interview should include information about the behavioral or interpersonal consequences of each problem rather than a global perception on the part of the patient. The severity of each problem, its frequency, its duration when it occurs, and past attempts to cope with the problem should all be evaluated to the extent possible. On the other hand, the therapist does not want to get bogged down in the early stages of an intake session because considerable additional information needs to be obtained. The assessment of problems should be comprehensive but also quick to allow for the collection of history and other information that is necessary in the early phase of treatment.

Once the problem list has been developed and the therapist and the patient have agreed with respect to the most important problems in the patient's life, the therapist will shift the focus of the first session to the collection of other important information: the personal history of the patient, his or her social development, schooling and occupational history, important social relationships, health history, and the history of the presenting problem in the context of other developmental issues. The therapist will also evaluate past coping efforts with the presenting problems, any treatments that the patient is involved in or may have attempted in the past, and the resources that the patient has at his or her disposal. In particular, if the past therapy was a model different from cognitive therapy, the therapist may comment about the difference between the current treatment and the past one to offset any negative biases the patient might have toward treatment in general.

One assessment strategy that has been recommended (Dobson & Dobson, 2009) is to ask the patient for a series of self-descriptive adjectives. If this task is done at the end of the assessment interview, the therapist can make some covert conjectures about what the patient will say and then contrast the patient's actual words with the therapist's predictions.

Agreement between the patient's self-descriptions and the therapist's predictions will help to demonstrate that the therapist's understanding of the patient is accurate. However, considerable discrepancies between the patient's self-descriptions and the therapist's predictions may suggest the need for further assessment or questioning by the therapist to better understand the patient's self-perceptions.

The therapist may need more information at the end of the initial interview. If so, additional testing can be conducted, records can be obtained from other therapists or other settings, conversations with significant other people in the patient's life can be held, and further interviews with the patient can be conducted. The therapist will want to have sufficient information to ensure that his or her case conceptualization is adequate to initiate treatment. On the other hand, a single intake interview will often yield enough material to generate at least a preliminary case conceptualization and to permit the start of treatment planning.

Case Conceptualization

The development of a case conceptualization is widely recognized to be a critical part of treatment planning in cognitive therapy (Persons, 1997, 2008). The development of a case formulation can be useful for

- developing a case model to understand the patient and his or her behavior,
- determining a priority sequence for solving problems,
- predicting optimal treatment strategies and which interventions not to use,
- developing the therapeutic relationship,
- anticipating treatment outcomes and setting realistic change targets, and
- understanding patient behavior over the course of therapy.

However, to be useful, a valid case conceptualization needs to meet several stringent criteria (Bieling & Kuyken, 2003). Specifically, it should have predictive validity, it should lead to improved outcomes relative to not having a conceptualization, it should improve the therapeutic alliance, and it should lead to enhanced treatment adherence by therapists. Research has not yet firmly concluded whether these criteria are met by most case conceptualizations (Kuyken, Fothergill, Musa, & Chadwick, 2005).

The heart of a case conceptualization is the description of the mechanism or mechanisms that the patient uses to create and maintain his or her problems. In this sense, a single patient may require distinct conceptualizations for the core beliefs that lie behind the problems that he or she presents in therapy. Since the cognitive model often involves a diathesis–stress process, in which the core beliefs represent the diathesis or vulnerability toward a problem and some life event or trigger is the stressor that precipitates the problems, the case formulation will usually delineate an interaction among one or more beliefs and one or more stressors. Once the process is begun, general behavioral strategies or behaviors such as avoidance may emerge, which in turn increase the likelihood of further stress, negative thinking, and the emotional and behavioral consequences of that negative thinking.

A case conceptualization can be diagrammed in a number of ways. The therapist can develop the first instance as a way to understand a new patient who is being evaluated. Over time, however, the patient is included in the development of the case formulation since he or she has information to elaborate certain elements or correct mistakes that the therapist may have made. As the case develops further, the therapist and patient together finalize the model and may develop experiments to gather information about less well-understood aspects of the case formulation.

A basic way to diagram the case conceptualization was presented in Figure 3.1. The bubble diagram is a concise form for sharing case conceptualizations and it is easily comprehended by most patients. It works best for single core beliefs. It does not present fully the process involved in most cases, as it does not include a space to conceptualize the developmental bases of the belief that is the focus of therapy. It also does not represent patterns of compensatory or maintenance behaviors that are employed by the patient to sustain his or her belief system. Thus, the bubble diagram may be more appropriate early in therapy, when the cognitive model is first described to the patient, then replaced with more elaborate models as the case develops.

Two other systems for case formulation have been widely promoted. Perhaps the best known was developed by Persons (Persons, 1989, 2008; Persons & Davidson, 2010). This formulation (see Figure 4.1) requires information about developmental considerations, current problems, core beliefs, stressors, the mechanisms that underlie the problems, and how these elements relate to each other. Case conceptualizations that use this model can include predictions about treatment goals, the strategies that seem to be indicated for the patient, planned techniques, and potential obstacles to treatment success.

The other major system for case conceptualization is by J. S. Beck (1995, 2005), as shown in Figure 4.2. This system incorporates most of the same information as the system developed by Persons, as it includes the childhood or developmental bases of the case, the schemas or beliefs that are the focus of therapy, and the triggers or stressors. It also incorporates conditional assumptions or rules that the patient has adopted, based on his or her belief system, and compensatory behavioral strategies. It does not include information about diagnosis and the patient's positive coping resources. This format for case conceptualization is used as a training and treatment resource in the Beck Institute and is "required" by therapists from the first session with a patient, despite the recognition that it evolves and becomes more complete with further contact and information gathering.

All three of the above case conceptualizations share certain elements. Among them are the need to articulate the core beliefs or schemas, the activating triggers for these schemas, and the resulting cognitive/behavioral/ emotional processes. These elements form the core features of the case conceptualization. Other aspects of the case, such as the historical determinants of the schema and maintenance strategies, are often critical pieces of information used in treatment planning. All formats recognize that the therapist and patient will both discover information to add to the case conceptualization over time. In this sense, the case conceptualization is an evolving model of the patient's functioning.

Which of the above three systems is the "correct" one to use will depend on circumstances. One will be more useful than the others for certain cases or for different phases of the same case. The bubble diagram could be used early in therapy, as it is simple and easy for most patients to

Patient Name:_____ Date:_____

Problem List:
1._____
2. _____
3. _____

DSM–IV Diagnosis:
Axis I._____
Axis II._____
Axis III._____
Axis IV._____
Axis V._____

Precipitants of the problem:

_____

Origins of the problem:

_____
_____

Core beliefs/schemas:

_____

Case formulation (origins, precipitants, mechanisms, problems):

_____
_____

Goals:
1._____
2. _____
3. _____

Modality:_____

Frequency:_____

Adjunct treatment(s):_____

Figure 4.1

Case formulation. From *Cognitive Therapy in Practice: A Case Formulation Approach* (p. 79), by J. B. Persons, 1989, New York, NY: Norton. Copyright 1989 by Norton; and *The Case Formulation Approach to Cognitive–Behavior Therapy* (p. 120), by J. B. Persons, 2008, New York, NY: Guilford Press. Copyright 2008 by Guilford Press. Adapted with permission.

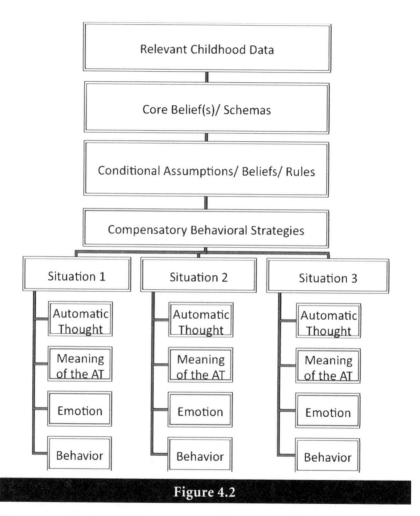

Figure 4.2

Case conceptualization model. From *Cognitive Therapy for Challenging Problems: What to Do When the Basics Don't Work* (p. 140), by J. S. Beck, 2005, New York, NY: Guilford Press. Copyright 2005 by J. S. Beck. Adapted with permission. AT = automatic thought.

understand. It could be replaced with something like the Beck format as the case becomes more complicated and its history clearer and after the therapist has witnessed schema activation in different situations. This format is also easy to teach to new cognitive therapists because it is comprehensive. Also, since it is similar to the case formulation model used by the Academy of Cognitive Therapy (http://www.academyofct.org), there is a linkage to the credentialing process for trainees with this aspiration. It does appear that the process of doing case conceptualizations can be trained and that with experience trainees will get closer to models in this area.

Socializing the Patient to Treatment

Another critical part of the early phases of cognitive therapy is to begin to teach the patient to think like a cognitive therapist. This is done in both explicit and subtle ways. For example, the therapist will use the cognitive model to explain the patient's problems back to him or her and thereby provide a cognitive case formulation. The formulation is not presented as a fact—the therapist and patient develop this model together over time— but as an explicit reference to the model and its predictions. Another explicit part of the socialization process is the introduction and use of different concepts and terms. For example, in common language, people often confuse terms related to cognition and emotion. However, the cognitive model posits that emotions generally follow from cognitive appraisals, and so clearly differentiating the words we use to describe how we think and feel and stating them in a manner that is consistent with the model helps the patient to learn how to use cognitive therapy techniques. In many cases, the therapist will spend time explaining different aspects of the cognitive model and even teaching terminology that will allow the patient to express himself or herself in a way that fits the model.

A number of terms are used in cognitive therapy that are not part of everyday language, such as *schema, cognitive distortion, attribution, cognitive error,* or the many terms used to describe the various types of distortions (e.g., *maximization, minimization, fortune telling, catastrophization*). The cognitive therapist should therefore use these terms judiciously and introduce them only when they are useful, and then define them and ensure that the patient understands them.

Socialization into the cognitive model takes place in subtle ways. When the patient presents different problems, the cognitive therapist will use language and explain the problem in cognitive terms. The therapist might say things like, "So what were you thinking just before you became angry?" This question implicitly reinforces the model that cognitions precede and predict emotional responses. As another example, after an effective cognitive restructuring exercise, the therapist might say something like, "So when you looked at this situation more objectively, it was not as scary as it had first seemed?" Such a question reinforces the idea that effective evidence gathering can undermine negative distortions, although not in an explicit manner. Indeed, many of the questions that therapists use in cognitive therapy have both an explicit element as well as a more subtle educative aspect. This type of "Socratic questioning" is similar to a series of leading questions in that the therapist wants the patient to come to some understanding through these questions, but they are open enough in their format that the therapist also learns about the patient through the responses. Socratic questioning is an interactional style that is used throughout cognitive therapy, and there is a general bias in cognitive therapy toward helping the patient arrive at his or her own solutions to the problems that are presented in therapy to facilitate the growth of self-efficacy and agency in the patient. However, questioning is not used in a dogmatic way. If the patient is truly stuck on an issue, the therapist may well provide information or guidance or may suggest how the patient can obtain help from other experts.

The End of the Beginning

The beginning stages of cognitive therapy are complex and multifaceted. The patient has a series of problems that are often acute, and he or she is frequently in distress. At the same time, the patient is trying to determine whether to invest time, energy, and trust in the therapist—that is, whether the therapist has the requisite knowledge, skills, experience, and trustworthiness. The therapist has to manage the legal and technical aspects of psychotherapy that are specific to his or her jurisdiction (e.g., informed consent, risk assessment). He or she is also gathering as much information as possible in as short a period of time as is practical. The therapist needs to develop a preliminary diagnosis and case conceptualization to determine whether the patient's problems fit into the cognitive model and to determine targets of change and likely interventions. The therapist also tries to make realistic assessments of the patient's history and prognosis, based on the information gathered and general knowledge of psychotherapy, to determine whether the patient is a good candidate for therapy. Ideally, the therapist does not just pay attention to the patient's statements but also thinks about what the science of psychopathology and psychotherapy have to contribute to the case. The therapist may consider additional assessment questions or techniques or consultation with other professionals if certain aspects of the patient's case are not clear. All the while, he or she strives to develop and maintain a good working relationship with the patient so that if the patient is accepted into therapy, the relationship begins on good footing.

Ideally, what emerges from all of the above is an initial agreement between therapist and patient about the problem or problems that will be targeted in therapy, a preliminary case conceptualization that is based on both general cognitive models and the specifics of the case, a beginning positive relationship that can develop over the course of time, and an initial general plan. As with any other system of psychotherapy, cognitive therapists are mindful that events may require a return to some of the more basic preliminary steps of treatment (e.g., the need for further assessment areas that emerge over the course of therapy, the need to address more fundamental aspects of the therapy relationship if a problem emerges, the need to assess safety or risk issues that might emerge), but in general treatment will proceed from the above steps.

AUTOMATIC THOUGHT WORK
IN COGNITIVE THERAPY

Many people consider the interventions described in this chapter to be the hallmarks of cognitive therapy. Indeed, many strategies to work with negative thinking are not described here (see, e.g., J. G. Dobson & Dobson, 2009; Leahy, 2003; McMullin, 2000). Although the interventions we

Automatic Thoughts

describe in this chapter focus on the cognitions that presumably are problematic in various disorders, a cognitive therapist is unlikely to work only with negative thoughts. Cognitive therapists are always interested in the effect of cognitive changes on other variables such as behavior and emotion. Furthermore, cognitive therapists are practical and want to see the effects of the techniques they use in the patient's day-to-day life. Cognitive interventions likely are conducted in concert with behavioral homework assignments and emotive techniques. Linking cognitive interventions with behavior and emotion ensures that the work has generalized effects rather than being simply an intellectual exercise. Conversely, it would be unusual for cognitive therapists to conduct behavior change experiments without examining the implications of behavioral change for cognition. Behavioral experiments are often used in cognitive therapy to reflect changes in cognition observed in the previous session, but those changes are also examined in the subsequent session to ensure that cognitive change occurs (K. S. Dobson & Hamilton, 2003).

Automatic Thoughts ∨ *Core Beliefs* The cognitive model distinguishes between situation-specific negative thoughts, which are also called *automatic thoughts,* and more traitlike or stable core beliefs and schemas. Conceptually, automatic thoughts are reactive to the moment and vary over time. Automatic thoughts can reflect appraisals of either an external event (e.g., becoming angry at another person's rude comment) or an internal state or reaction (e.g., noticing that one is tired and becoming afraid that another episode of depression is coming on). Automatic thoughts can be directly tied to events (e.g., becoming anxious when seeing a picture of a large snake) or can reflect appraisals about appraisals (e.g., thinking that one is foolish for being fearful of a picture of a snake). The latter process has also been referred to as *metacognition,* a second-order appraisal through which some meaning or importance is attached to an experience (Emmelkamp & Aardema, 1999; Wells, 2002; Wells & Sembi, 2004).

Automatic thoughts occur all of the time and can be attended to almost as a second stream of consciousness. Automatic thoughts are either neutral or positive for many people, but everyone has negative thoughts. It has been estimated that the average ratio of positive to negative thoughts in healthy people is 2:1 (Kendall, Howard, & Hays, 1989). In the case of the various disorders, automatic thoughts reflect core beliefs and are often negative in nature. For example, patients with anxiety disorders often have many specific fears and worries that arise spontaneously over the course of a day. People with depression may be self-denigrating and critical of their own actions. People with eating disorders may often find that they worry about their body shape and wish that it were different. These are the automatic thoughts that can be the focus of the interventions discussed in this chapter.

Two broad classes of interventions are used to work with negative automatic thoughts. In some cases, the patients' perceptions are more negative than the situations warrant or the perception may be a distorted one. In these instances, interventions that try to change negative thoughts can be approached from the perspective of the evidence that either supports or refutes the automatic thought. If the evidence does not support the negative thought, the patient can be invited to revise his or her ideas. Automatic thoughts can be first considered from the perspective of the alternative ways in which a person could view or react to a given situation regardless of the facts. For example, if a patient has become indignant in response to a perceived slight, it may be more helpful to get him or her to recognize alternative ways to understand his or her anger and indignation than to attempt to justify the original thought.

Whether the interventions are based on the encouragement of realistic thinking or of alternative thinking, the therapist's ability to engage with the patient around the *process* of thinking itself, or what is sometimes referred to as *cognitive restructuring* (Dobson & Dobson, 2009), is key. The cognitive model posits that as patients learn to modify the process of thinking, they will also change the outcomes associated with their thoughts. In a typical case of cognitive therapy, most of the therapist's time will be spent in teaching techniques related to changing automatic thoughts, examining homework related to the interventions, and ensuring that the skills are well established before the end of treatment.

Although it is possible to begin to work to change automatic thoughts early in the process of cognitive therapy, cognitive therapists will often want to spend some time educating patients about their negative automatic thoughts and how the thoughts affect the quality of their lives. For example, the therapist might note a negative thought in the first or second session and inquire about the evidence that the patient uses to justify the thought. Depending on the information that the patient provides, a therapist might ask the patient to recall additional specifics of the situation, perhaps by queuing other memories about the event. The therapist may evoke clearer memories by asking the patient to close his or her eyes and to recall the circumstances. In some cases, homework might be used to clarify memories: The patient asks the other person in the situation what their recollection of the event is, and the patient can reconcile his or her memories with those of the other person. The therapist may develop a homework assignment in which the patient purposely recreates the situation to see what types of automatic thoughts emerge. Or the therapist might simply encourage the patient to notice the thoughts that he or she has the next time the situation occurs.

Assessment of Automatic Thoughts

Various methods can be used to collect information about automatic thoughts. If the thought is relatively simple and repetitive, recording its frequency might be sufficient. In such cases even something as simple as a golf counter can be used to collect frequency information. The thought can be monitored and may become less frequent as it is challenged over the course of therapy. If the thought is more complex, the patient may maintain a small notebook or ledger in which he or she can record the thoughts. The actual content of the thought thus can be examined and may change over the course of treatment. The following presents a brief interaction between therapist and patient, which illustrates how a cognitive therapist might try to orient a female patient to the role that negative automatic thoughts play in emotional distress:

Patient: I had a real fright last night, when my ex-husband called and said our son was hurt.

Therapist: What happened?

Patient: Nothing much really, but when he called he said that Nicholas, our son, had been in an accident. My first thought was that he was dead or at least in the hospital, the way he said it.

Therapist: So you quickly jumped to the worst possible thing?

Patient: Yes, that happens pretty often. But then when I found out that he had only cut himself at the playground I thought that maybe my ex was just putting things in a dramatic way to get me going. He is like that.

Therapist: I take it that you have other experiences with him where maybe he tried to get you upset?

Patient: Yes, whenever I talk with him now, I am always on my guard.

Therapist: So, in this case you both had a tendency to hear the worst about your child and to imagine the worst about your ex-husband! It's probably not too surprising that you had a real fright.

As noted in the last section, cognitive therapy often has an educational aspect. In some cases it is appropriate to directly instruct the patient about the cognitive model and to explain the relationships among beliefs, triggers, automatic thoughts, and the emotional and behavioral consequences of negative thoughts. Some patients may want to read more about the process, and the therapist can assign a workbook such as *Mind Over Mood* (Greenberger & Padesky, 1995) or a text such as *Reinventing Your Life* (Young & Klosko, 1994). Furthermore, patients can be instructed about the various types of negative thoughts related to distress and the various forms of distortions. If it seems appropriate and the patient is interested, he or she can be provided with a list of common cognitive distortions (see Table 4.1). Some patients enjoy discussing how their experience can be biased by distortions that fit with core beliefs, and some patients even enjoy identifying their own distortive tendencies as a kind of investigative process.

The content of the thought, the context in which it arises, and the consequences of the thought are important. Thought records are commonly used to capture this information. The dysfunctional thought record (DTR) was initially developed (A. T. Beck, Rush, Shaw, & Emery, 1979) to assess the automatic thoughts of depressed patients; however, the DTR is generally useful in the assessment of automatic thoughts across a range of problems.

Table 4.1

Common Cognitive Distortions

Distortion	Description
All-or-nothing thinking	Viewing a situation as having only two possible outcomes; also called *black-and-white* or *dichotomous* thinking
Catastrophization	Predicting future calamity; ignoring a possible positive future
Fortune-telling	Predicting the future with limited evidence
Mind reading	Predicting or believing you know what other people think
Disqualifying the positive	Not attending to or giving due weight to positive information; similar to a negative tunnel vision
Magnification/minimization	Magnifying negative information; minimizing positive information
Selective abstraction	Focusing on one detail rather than the big picture; also called *mental filter*
Overgeneralization	Drawing overstated conclusions based on one or a limited number of instances
Misattribution	Making errors in the attribution of causes of various events
Personalization	Thinking that negative things are due to you rather than examining other causes
Emotional reasoning	Arguing that because something feels bad, it must be bad
Labeling	Putting a general label on someone or something rather than describing the behaviors or aspects of the thing

Note. From *Cognitive Therapy: Basics and Beyond* (p. 119), by J. S. Beck, 1995, New York, NY: Guilford Press. Copyright 1995 by Guilford Press. Adapted with permission.

Several variants of the DTR have been developed. The original DTR (A. T. Beck et al., 1979) had several columns (see Figure 4.3). The first column is for noting date and time of the problematic situation. The second column is for a brief description of the situation, or if there was no external situation, the internal memory or experience that led to the negative automatic thoughts. The third column is for recording the emotional consequence of the automatic thought, which is not only named but also typically given a severity rating on a scale of 0 to 100. The final column is for listing the automatic thoughts and for rating believability on a scale of 0 to 100.

Figure 4.3 shows an example of the type of information that can be collected on the DTR. As shown in the figure, the patient identified a dif-

Date/time	Situation (actual event or memory)	Emotion(s) (Intensity rating, 0–100)	Automatic thoughts (Believability rating, 0–100)
Friday, 4:30 p.m.	Getting ready to leave work for the weekend. No particular plans.	Sad (50) Lonely (70) Angry (40)	I hate the weekend. (90) No one cares about me. (85) Why can't I find people to hang out with? (40) I'm lonely. (80)

Figure 4.3

Original dysfunctional thought record.

ficult situation and recorded her emotional experiences. The automatic thoughts are generally consistent with the emotional experiences that she recorded, although some do not seem tied to the emotions that were listed. In the example "Why can't I find people to hang out with?" it is unclear what thought or image might have been behind the anger reaction. In such a case, the cognitive therapist would likely inquire further. First, the therapist would get a detailed description of the event to be able to imagine himself or herself in the situation. Second, the therapist would ask for more information about the emotional experiences and the severity. Often the therapist will distinguish among the first and subsequent reactions to distinguish the primary emotional experience from any secondary reactions. Finally, the therapist will help the patient in recalling the thoughts he or she had in the situation (not the patient's ideas of what thoughts they might have or should have had). Again, the most strongly held or primary automatic thought may be distinguished from secondary metacognitions or from less important automatic thoughts. It might be helpful to draw lines on the DTR to connect different automatic thoughts with the emotional consequences that they engendered.

The original form of the DTR has some limitations. First, it fails to place the hypothetical relationship among variables in their proper sequence. According to the cognitive model, different emotional reactions result from the automatic thoughts that arise in varying situations. A conceptually more appropriate format for the DTR would be one in which the situation is listed first, followed by the automatic thoughts, and then the emotional consequences. Second, the original DTR does not provide a column for the behavioral consequences of different negative automatic thoughts. Although patients often focus on the content and valence of their emotional reactions to different situations or triggers, the cognitive model of change invokes behavioral strategies as part of the interventions. Knowing the patient's typical behavioral responses to negative automatic thoughts can be important in helping the therapist plan the appropriate interventions. A more theoretically consistent and complete form of the DTR might therefore be the one that is presented in Figure 4.4. In this case, the avoidance behaviors that are identified may become important because the lack of planning by the patient may create a self-fulfilling prophecy in which he or she dislikes weekends because of their meaning and emotional emptiness, but then fails to make plans that could reduce that response pattern.

Working With Automatic Thoughts

Once the patient begins to notice and record the automatic thoughts that occur in different situations, the therapist encourages him or her to bring

Date/time	Situation (actual event or memory)	Automatic thought(s) (Believability rating, 0–100)	Emotions (Intensity Rating, 0–100)	Behaviors
Friday, 4:30 p.m.	Getting ready to leave work for the weekend. No particular plans.	I hate the weekend. (90) No one cares about me. (85) Why can't I find people to hang out with? (40) I'm lonely. (80)	Sad (50) Lonely (70) Angry (40)	Delaying leaving work. Avoiding making any plans for the weekend.

Figure 4.4

Modified dysfunctional thought record.

them into treatment. The therapist needs to support this activity because simply exposing the thoughts can be difficult for the patient. For example, if some of the patient's thoughts have little evidence to substantiate them, he or she may be afraid to write them down for fear that the therapist will think them foolish. Some patients can see ways in which their thoughts are illogical or "wrong," and they might try to quickly change or suppress certain thoughts and not give the therapist the chance to fully understand their thought process. The therapist should treat the thought records factually and in an investigative manner. The therapist should communicate the desire to understand the patient without judgment about the patient's thought patterns. Sometimes it is important for the therapist to explain to the patient the value of recording accurate and complete information so that the interventions that will best help the patient can be planned.

One of the virtues of cognitive therapy is the multitude of interventions that are available for working with negative thoughts (D. J. G. Dobson & Dobson, 2009; Leahy, 2003; McMullin, 2000; W. O'Donohue & Fisher, 2008). Because most patients have many negative automatic thoughts, the selection of the most useful intervention for a given automatic thought can be daunting for beginning therapists.

The thoughts connected with the most distressing situation (the "hot cognitions") should be chosen for interventions. In addition, cognitive therapists generally focus on the most distressing or dysfunctional automatic thought within any given situation. Cognitive therapists try to solve problems as efficiently as possible even at the level of within-session decisions about targets of intervention. Picking the most distressing situation from a DTR and working it through fully is generally more effective than addressing several negative thoughts more superficially. If other difficult situations or thoughts exist, they will likely recur on a future thought record and can be worked on at that time.

The above discussion regarding the collection of automatic thoughts demonstrates that no one ideal or preferred method for doing this work exists in cognitive therapy. Patients can self-report their automatic thoughts, collect counts of automatic thoughts, use forms, write notes to themselves on a pad or paper diary, use an electronic diary, or create spreadsheets or notepads in their personal computers. The important principle is that these thoughts are attended to and reported in therapy sessions so that the therapist can understand the patient's thoughts and plan an intervention program. Although certain patterns of automatic thoughts are typical of patients with the same diagnoses or problems, every person is an individual, and understanding the particular mechanisms by which each patient experiences his or her problems is a critical part of the therapeutic process.

Intervening With Automatic Thoughts

Once automatic thoughts are being consistently reported in treatment, appropriate interventions can be selected. Three broad classes of interventions for negative automatic thoughts can be distinguished by the manner in which the patient might answer the following three questions:

1. What evidence supports or does not support the automatic thought?
2. What are the viable alternative thoughts in this situation?
3. What meaning is attached to the automatic thought?

The interventions associated with each of these three questions are discussed next.

Evidence-Based Interventions for Automatic Thoughts

In general, the first set of interventions that a cognitive therapist will consider relates to the match or mismatch between the automatic thought and the situation or trigger. Patients with various diagnoses characteristically distort or misperceive events or their own experiences in a manner that is consistent with their core beliefs and current problems. For example, patients with anxiety tend to overstate the danger of situations they face or might underestimate their ability to cope. Angry people often overstate the intention of another person with little supporting evidence. Therefore, identifying distorted or exaggerated thoughts is a regular feature of cognitive therapy for various disorders.

The general belief in cognitive therapy is that patients perceive the world and themselves in a manner consistent with their core beliefs and schemas. As described in Chapter 3, schemas not only affect how we view events that have already occurred but also lead us to look for information in new situations that is consistent with our core beliefs and to engage in different behaviors that tend to reinforce our beliefs. Also as noted previously, the cognitive model presumes that real events occur and may be perceived accurately or be distorted. The degree of discrepancy between the actual event and the perception of it is a direct reflection of the degree of psychopathology experienced by the patient.

If the therapist comes to understand that the patient is engaging in cognitive distortions, either through reviewing thought records or other analyses of the negative thoughts that the patient brings to therapy, he or she may discuss the process of cognitive distortions with the patient. The therapist would educate the patient about the proactive nature of core beliefs and note that distortion is a normal process for anyone with a particular set of core beliefs. For example, a woman with social anxiety disorder likely has the perception that other people are critical, which leads her to reduce her social engagement, to perceive criticism from other people when it may not be intended, and generally to perpetuate her belief about the critical nature of others. Providing a rationale of this type to patients can allow them to understand why they might distort social interactions. An understanding of this process can also help patients in searching for distortive processes in the future.

A cognitive therapist who chooses to intervene in cognitive distortions might provide the patient with a list of cognitive distortions (see Table 4.1 for an example) and a definition of each distortion. The patient might then be encouraged to examine his or her automatic thoughts and to explore with the therapist whether any of these thoughts are distorted. Some patients enjoy this investigative process, which can allow them to distance themselves from the momentary experience of the situation and to look at the "facts of the matter" more dispassionately. Some patients enjoy the process of labeling their own cognitive distortions because it gives them a shorthand way to think about their negative thought processes.

If the patient demonstrates a clear and repeated type of cognitive distortion, the cognitive therapist might discuss it at length with the patient. For example, many patients with anxiety disorders engage in fortune-telling and make negative predictions about what will happen if they confront their feared object or situation. The therapist can discuss the cognitive, emotional, and behavioral consequences of negative fortune-telling, and once the patient concurs, the therapist and patient can design a behavioral experiment to test the predictions that are being made by the patient. In the case of depression, a characteristic cognitive distortion is that of making negative attributions for failure (in particular, blaming oneself for negative outcomes). If the therapist observes this attributional pattern, he or she can spend time with the patient in observing the facts of the situation to determine whether negative attributions are warranted.

A number of specific interventions have been developed for the evidence-based approach to negative automatic thoughts. In some cases, the intervention consists of asking the patient for more details about the trigger or situation that precipitated the negative thoughts. The therapist then listens for distortions in the patient's perceptions and through a series of questions contrasts the facts of the matter with the perceptions. If skillfully done, this type of Socratic questioning will identify for the patient where he or she has exaggerated or misperceived the situation and will allow the patient to modify the automatic thoughts to be more consistent with the facts. In instances where insufficient evidence exists to fully judge the accuracy of the thought, homework may be developed to collect more information.

Negative fortune-telling is a common distortion. Often, based on the negative prediction, a patient may fail to engage in a particular social task or other behavior; indeed, avoidance patterns almost always have some degree of negative fortune-telling associated with them. For example, a patient who expects his partner to get angry with him in certain situations may purposely avoid getting into those situations. When this type of negative automatic thought emerges, the patient can undertake a homework assignment in which he or she makes a prediction (ideally, a specific and time-limited prediction that can be evaluated against the evidence), then goes out and collects information to evaluate the accuracy of the prediction. Such assignments are ideal in the context of cognitive therapy because they may identify exaggerated negative predictions by the patient and allow the patient to modify such predictions in the future. In instances where the outcome is partially negative, graduated thinking and degrees of success or failure can be discussed. And even in instances where the outcomes are as negative as the patient had predicted, the patient can still congratulate himself or herself for having explored the situation that has been previously avoided. In addition, knowing the actual outcomes will allow the therapist and patient to discuss more effective problem-solving strategies for use in the future.

As noted above, another fairly common type of cognitive distortion is negative attribution. Negative attributions occur regularly in patients with depression: They often blame themselves for perceived failure. Negative attributions also emerge in anger-related problems when the patient makes negative attributions toward other people in the social environment (e.g., "He did it to me, and on purpose"). Attributional biases are relatively easy to evaluate using evidence-based strategies. In the context of depression, overly negative attributions for failure can often be identified. Sometimes just drawing such biases to the attention of patients with depression can allow them to examine other causes for different outcomes and to blame themselves less for failure. As they make positive changes during treatment, depressed patients can use positive attributional biases to give themselves credit for the advances that they have made. Indeed, a general strategy in cognitive therapy is to encourage internal attributions for positive changes made over the course of therapy.

Labeling is yet another type of cognitive distortion that lends itself to an evidence-based intervention. People engage in labeling as a shorthand way to describe themselves or others. Labels are often extreme and, almost by definition, categorical. When the cognitive therapist hears a patient engaging in labeling, he or she can undertake a series of interventions. First, the therapist may inquire about the actual behaviors or attributes of a person that the patient uses as cues to make the label. Often a particular feature or behavior is being noted and other aspects of a person's behavior are ignored. Developing a broader perception of a person may undermine the labeling process. Second, the process of asking about the actual behaviors allows for a more complete description of the person, including not only the associated negative attributes but also his or her positive attributes or characteristics. Third, when the behaviors rather than the label are described, it often becomes clear that the person does not *always* do whatever the patient has noticed in applying the label. The awareness of variability allows for discussion about the extent to which that person engages in various activities and for a more graduated and evidence-based perception of the person.

Evidence-based strategies have recently been used with regard to delusions. Whereas in the past it was thought that formal delusional experiences could not be evaluated (since by definition they are out of contact with reality), more recent clinical experience and trials have shown that delusions can be subjected to evidence-based intervention (A. T. Beck et al., 2009). This type of intervention follows a series of steps: The particular delusional belief is identified, its consequences are named, predictions based on the delusional belief are made, and then evidence-based strategies are used to test the predictions. Recent clinical work suggests that evidence-based approaches can undermine the confidence that patients have in their deluded beliefs and, if the experiment is effective, can undermine a delusional idea (Kingdon & Turkington, 2005).

The following dialogue exemplifies how a cognitive therapist might work with a patient using evidence-based techniques:

Therapist: As you speak, I get the impression that you might sometimes not just react to the situation you are in, but also to your own way of thinking about things.

Patient: I'm not sure what you mean.

Therapist: Well, earlier you told me that you started to cry when you heard that your friend may have cancer.

Patient: Yes, of course.

Therapist: So what idea did you have, do you think, that made you so sad?

Patient: I imagined her husband and their children trying to get by without her. She has always been the strength in the family, and I just can't imagine them doing very well.

Therapist: So, in your mind, it is like you already have your friend dead and buried. But what did she actually tell you? Did she say she had cancer?

Patient: Well, no, not exactly. She told me she had a lump in her breast, and that she was going to see her doctor right away. I know that breast cancer is pretty serious.

Therapist: Do women have this problem without having cancer?

Patient: I suppose so.

Therapist: And if it was breast cancer, what is the survival rate?

Patient: I don't actually know.

Therapist: So, I think that I understand your compassion and concern about your friend and her family, but is it possible that you have maybe overreacted to what you actually know?

Patient: Well, when you put it this way, I guess so. But I was really upset, so naturally I just thought of the worst possibility.

In all of the evidence-based strategies listed above, it is insufficient for the therapist to have the evidence to undermine a given negative automatic thought. It is imperative for the patient to recognize the evidence that is needed to undermine the thought. An effective question that can be asked of the patient in designing experiments or evaluating evidence is, "What information or evidence would it take for you to change your mind?" Having elaborated the patient's requirement for evidence to modify the automatic thought, the therapist and patient can then work to that end. For the therapist to simply contradict the patient's automatic thoughts or to tell him or her the "truth" about a matter is rarely of much use because the patient's perspective is the critical ingredient in changing the emotional and behavioral outcomes of the initial perception.

Alternative-Based Interventions

The second class of interventions in working with negative thoughts is the examination of alternatives. In some cases, having reviewed the evidence related to a negative automatic thought, it becomes apparent that the original thought is not justified. The patient can be asked for a more accurate rendition of the situation. A simple strategy to urge this type of alternative thinking is to inquire whether the patient can think about the event in another way. The tactic of encouraging alternative perspectives may illustrate for the patient how locked in and rigid certain types of thinking are. This exercise allows patients to look at the situation from another person's perspective or from their own perspective as if they were not as distressed.

A more formal strategy to encourage alternative responses to negative automatic thoughts is the rational role-play in which the therapist asks the patient to state out loud his or her automatic thoughts. The therapist then verbalizes each statement and encourages the patient to respond, similar in form to a debate or a role-play among alternative thoughts. If the patient struggles with this exercise, the therapist may role-play the alternative responses to the original negative thoughts to provide possible ways to "talk back" to these thoughts. The therapist should assess the believability of these alternatives so that the patient can either accept or reject them. If the therapist does take the step of responding to the negative automatic thoughts, it is necessary to reverse this role-play so that the patient has the opportunity to respond in an alternative manner to his or her original negative thoughts. This type of role-play exercise can be repeated across sessions until the patient is fluent with the process of responding to negative thoughts. The rational role-play technique can incorporate elements of an evidence-based response, but the alternatives must be credible to the patient, even if no evidence exists to support or refute the alternative thoughts.

Another strategy to examine reasonable alternatives to negative automatic thoughts involves homework in which the patient identifies *possible* alternative thoughts, even in the absence of particular evidence and even if the alternatives do not seem credible. The homework assignment is not to find out whether the original thought was true but rather to poll friends and colleagues about alternative ways to view the situation. The strategy of polling encourages the patient to learn about perspectives that may be viable alternatives to the original negative thought. If the therapist is aware of a particular resource or system to capture such alternatives, this kind of perspective taking might be extended by using various media or other information sources. For example, in *Feeling Good* (Burns, 1980), different types of alternative perspectives are provided for difficult thoughts in several chapters. In addition, movies or books might aid in this type of perspective taking.

Another strategy for generating alternatives to negative thoughts is to treat the process as a problem-solving exercise. In problem-solving therapy (D'Zurilla & Nezu, 2007), the technique for overcoming problems involves generating as many ways to solve a problem as possible. During problem solving, the patient is encouraged to withhold any judgments about the "correct" or optimal response until the largest possible number of alternatives has been generated. In like fashion, cognitive therapists can encourage the patient to generate many alternative thoughts to the particular situation, and the therapist and patient can together review the viability of the alternative perspectives. This exercise also can be useful in assessing the patient's ability to think about situations in different ways. If necessary, the therapist can prompt or encourage different ways of thinking about situations. In general, however, a cognitive therapist will tend not to provide alternative perspectives unless the patient is willing to entertain the suggestions as reasonable alternatives. Again, the purpose of looking at alternative thoughts is not to generate ideas that the therapist can believe but rather to develop alternatives that are credible to the patient.

The use of humor is another strategy to encourage alternative perspectives to a negative thought. Jokes and humor often require a sudden shift in perspective. For example, many jokes are set up so that the listener expects a certain kind of dialogue or communication; a twist in perspective or radical shift in what is being communicated creates humor. If the therapeutic relationship is sound and if patients have shown any predilection toward humor, subtle jokes about the patients' original negative thoughts can encourage them to look at alternatives. If humor is used as a cognitive therapy technique, being clear that the humor is directed toward the thoughts rather than the patients is critical. Belief by patients that the therapist is making fun of them or is not taking their problems seriously can lead to a therapeutic rupture. Humor should be used judiciously and typically later in the process of therapy, once the patient is feeling better than when he or she first came to therapy and when the therapist is confident in the therapeutic relationship.

Another technique to encourage alternative thoughts is to ask the patient how useful or adaptive the original negative thought was. The intent is not to look at the accuracy or the viability of the negative thought but rather at its value or utility in the patient's life. In some cases, a negative thought might be accurate, but holding on to it is not helpful with respect to the patient's ongoing relationships or longer term personal goals (e.g., "Yes, he hurt your pride. How helpful is it, though, to harbor resentment toward men in general? Doesn't this reaction get in the way of making new relationships?"). In such cases, patients can be asked about the value of retaining this thought to encourage them to hold on to it less tightly so that alternative thoughts can be entertained.

The question about the value of holding on to a particular thought may lead to a broader discussion about the meaning that the thought has for the patient. A patient may say that he cannot let go of a particular thought even though he knows that it is problematic because to do so would have a particular meaning for him. For example, a patient might hang on to hurt feelings that were precipitated by a relationship rejection long after the other person has started new relationships. On inquiry, it may turn out that he has this reaction because giving up hurt feelings would signal to him that the relationship is over and that he is alone. The discussion can then lead to a deeper discussion about the meanings associated with particular negative thoughts, as is described below.

Emotional reasoning is a type of negative thought that lends itself to an examination of alternatives. Emotional reasoning occurs when people use their emotional response to a situation to justify the automatic thought that led to the response. For example, after an altercation the patient may say "I felt horrible, so she must have really insulted me badly." If the therapist hears this type of distortion, the logical error of affirming an antecedent based on a consequence can be discussed. The therapist can also use this opportunity to generate alternative thoughts or reactions to the situation as thought experiments. For example, the therapist can ask questions such as "How might somebody else have responded to this situation?" or "How might you have responded to this situation, if you weren't feeling the way that you are at present?" The therapist can help the patient recognize that thoughts do not establish facts; thoughts are just thoughts and can be evaluated in their own right.

Which of the above methods is most effective in generating credible alternatives to the original negative thought? Unfortunately, discovering which of these interventions will be effective with a particular patient, or at what time over the course of therapy it will be effective, is often a matter of trial and error. Fortunately, cognitive therapists have generated many interventions, so if one attempt does not work, an alternative strategy may be effective. Sometimes it is useful to step back from the actual interventions and discuss with the patient the general idea of looking at the evidence and the alternatives to negative thoughts. Such a discussion has an educational aspect and provides a framework for the patient to think about his or her negative thoughts. The discussion also signals the therapist's desire to help the patient develop more adaptive ways to respond to difficult situations and to give the patient the freedom to approach difficult people and situations in more productive ways.

Cognitive restructuring techniques such as those described above often can be done through simple therapeutic dialogue—the thrust and parry of verbal exchange in psychotherapy. However, it is also possible to formalize these strategies through written experiments. A number of techniques have been developed in this regard. For example, a relatively easy strategy for looking at alternative thoughts is through the use of a flash card. If the patient has a repetitive negative thought or behavioral pattern to which a more adaptive and viable alternative can be generated, the original negative thought can be written on the top part of the flash card and the more viable alternative on the bottom. The card can be posted in a visible location for the patient, such as on the refrigerator at home or on a bulletin board at work, so that when the original negative thought occurs, the alternative is readily available. A similar technique is called TIC-TOC. In TIC-TOC, if a patient has a recurring negative thought that can be counteracted by a viable and reasonable alternative, the patient can be encouraged to think about the image of a pendulum clock, so that when the first TIC (task-interfering cognition) occurs, it can be replaced with a TOC (task-oriented cognition).

Perhaps the best-known formal technique for modifying automatic thoughts is the use of an expanded DTR. Figure 4.5 presents an example of a complete DTR. Columns have been added for the identification of cognitive distortions in the figure, the correction of negative thoughts (which can be achieved through evidence review, the generation of reasonable alternatives, or a combination), and the emotional and behavioral outcomes of the alternative thoughts. This type of DTR allows the patient and therapist to work through various difficult situations and negative thoughts, to explore them fully, and to formally write down the method

Date/time	Situation	Automatic thoughts (Believability rating, 0–100)	Emotions (Intensity rating, 0–100)	Behaviors	Distortions	Responses to automatic thoughts (Believability rating, 0–100)	Emotions (Intensity rating, 0–100)	Behaviors
May 17, 8:30 p.m.	My husband was home late from work again, after saying he would not be. This is the fifth time this month.	Where is he? (50)	Anxiety (50)			I do not know. (100)	Anxiety (50)	Reading a book with the TV on in the background.
		He is having an affair. (85)	Anger (50) Sadness 30		Arbitrary inference	I do not have any evidence to know. He seems loving enough when home. (80)	Anger (30)	
		Maybe he has had an accident. (25)	Anxiety (20)	Watching TV for accident reports.	Arbitrary inference	If there was an accident, the police would phone. (70)	Worry (10)	
		His work is too demanding. (60)	Anger (50)		Maximization Ignoring the positive	He says he enjoys his work. (90)	Anger (20)	
		If he loved me, he would at least call. (90)	Sadness (50) Loneliness (70) Anger (80)	Check to see if phone line is working.	Arbitrary inference	Phoning would not prove his love for me. (80)	Loneliness (40) Love (50)	

Figure 4.5

Completed dysfunctional thought record.

for changing these thoughts. In many cases of cognitive therapy, several sessions will be spent working through DTRs to ensure that the patient has the techniques well in hand. In addition to having these forms preprinted, free-form diary formats, handwritten sheets, or computerized thought records may be used. Regardless of the type of form, the key is to have the methods readily available for use by patients. The cognitive therapist should use the format that will work in the patient's life.

Developing Positive Thoughts

The interventions described so far have focused on the identification and reduction of negative thoughts. Cognitive therapists also encourage the development of positive thoughts. For example, if a mother expresses the thought, "I worry that my child will become sick and I won't know what to do," the therapist could focus on the worry-related thoughts and sense of incompetence that generate this emotional response. However, this type of worry can be generated by a deep concern and love for one's child and a desire to protect the child from harm. Thus the therapist could focus on the positive aspect of the cognition and help the patient develop alternative ways of expressing her love and concern rather than worrying. This type of intervention is sometimes referred to as *reframing* and can be effective if the patient is open to this alternative way of thinking about a situation.

A discussion of negative thoughts and their effects can be used as a springboard to a discussion of the effects of positive thoughts. Patients can be encouraged to experiment with positive thoughts in their day-to-day lives to enable them to see what emotional and behavioral consequences are engendered. For example, a depressed patient may have learned that simple actions, even if they do not overcome an entire problem, lead to positive emotions and a sense of progress. The patient could generate a summary statement such as "I just need to try." The statement could be written on a flash card or in some other reminder system that the patient could use when confronted with a difficult task. The positive statement is not the same as a self-affirmation (McMullin, 2000) because the positive statement is based on the patient's own experience and will have a particular meaning for him or for her. A positive thought needs to resonate with or be believable to the patient at some level before it is used in homework or other assignments.

Meaning-Based Interventions

The third class of interventions used in working with automatic thoughts is the examination of the meanings attached to or the inferences that are drawn from different experiences. Often the inferences are themselves automatic thoughts, which are about either other thoughts or the emotional and behavioral consequences of the thoughts. These metacognitions are in effect another level of thought and are generated in response to the original automatic thought and the related experiences. For example, a single man may attend a social event and approach someone whom he finds attractive, only to be rebuffed. The experience might lead to automatic thoughts such as "I am not very attractive to others" or "I made a fool of myself." Once the thoughts emerge, the patient may experience embarrassment, and when he notices, he might generate secondary thoughts such as "I am a social misfit" or "Why would anyone want to be with me when I am so easily embarrassed?" These secondary automatic thoughts, or metacognitions, might be generated from either the same core beliefs that prompted the initial thought or from a related but deeper level of belief or schema.

When a cognitive therapist asks the patient questions about the meanings or inferences that have been drawn from automatic thoughts, the discussion often moves from situation-specific thinking to more general and trait-like patterns of thought. The technique, known as the *downward arrow* (J. S. Beck, 1995), has been well documented. Rather than disputing or challenging negative thoughts, the therapist asks the patient to assume that the first automatic thought is true or valid, then further queries the patient about the inference or conclusion that he or she has drawn. The therapist's question can be described as the "So what?" question, as in "So what if your thought is true? What would that mean about you?" The patient's response is then questioned in the same way, and the patient draws increasingly broad implications until it seems that a final, "deepest" meaning or inference is obtained. Figure 4.6 presents an example of the downward arrow for a college student who may have failed her midterm examination.

76

Student patient:	Therapist:
I think I failed my biology examination yesterday.	
	You seem pretty distressed by this idea. If you did fail this exam, what would that mean?
It means I will fail the course and probably have to drop out of college.	
	And for the moment, let's assume that was so. What would that mean about you?
It would mean I will not get a degree, and not be able to get the kind of job I want.	
	And if so? I mean, how would that affect you or your life?
My parents would know what a failure I am, and so would everyone else. I would not be able to hold my head up anymore.	
	I see. And again, if that were true, what would it mean?
I would be exposed as the failure I probably am.	
	And as bad as that probably seems, imagine for the moment that you are exposed. What implications would that outcome have for you?
I am a failure in life. I might as well give up right now.	
	OK—so the possibility of a single failure on an exam has some pretty significant implications for you! Let's go back and evaluate how justified these worries might be.

Figure 4.6

Example of the downward arrow technique.

The downward arrow is an easy technique to learn and apply. It is also an efficient way to expose the core beliefs that lie beneath negative automatic thoughts. If used too early in the therapy, the downward arrow can reveal belief systems for which the patient has no ready response and can increase patient distress and despondency. The therapist always begins the downward arrow with a preface, such as, "Well, I am not sure if your thought is accurate or not. But I wonder if I could ask you some questions about what it would mean if it were true? These questions will help us both to better understand the importance of these ideas for you." This disclaimer allows the therapist to backtrack after completing the downward arrow to do other interventions such as exploring the evidence related to the initial automatic thought.

Working with thoughts at the level of meanings often leads directly into assessment of and intervention with core beliefs and schemas. The timing of these interventions involves a major clinical judgment. Some patients come to therapy with fairly evident beliefs, which are clearly related to their presenting problems. Some patients come to cognitive therapy having had a course of another form of psychotherapy that has led to some degree of insight, such that the patient seems ready to work directly on core beliefs. In some cases the therapist may be seduced into discussion about core beliefs, only to later find that the discussion leads to a lack of action on the patient's part and to growing frustration on the therapist's part. Doing the more fundamental behavioral and automatic thought work is often a necessary precursor to working with beliefs. The time and effort spent on behavioral and automatic thought change permit the therapist to know the patient well, to socialize the patient into change, to ready the patient for belief change, and to ensure that the patient is motivated to make such changes. As described in Chapter 5, changing beliefs is difficult and is often met with resistance. The cognitive therapy model proposes that lasting change will be most associated with changes in beliefs, which are detailed in the next section.

WORKING WITH CORE BELIEFS AND SCHEMAS

As described in a previous chapter, the cognitive therapy model assumes that everyone has beliefs or schemas that they "carry around inside their minds." Although the precise mechanisms by which this happens are unknown, individuals are presumed to be born with a tendency to organize their experiences and the information that they encounter in the world. The architecture of cognitive organization is more or less universal and automatic, but the content of a person's beliefs and schemas primarily are dictated by life experiences. Cognitive psychology has provided key information about the processes by which individuals develop functional or dysfunctional beliefs and schemas. Clinical cognitive psychopathology combines broad theoretical frameworks with the ideographic processes that have led to the patient's distress and problems in adaptive coping.

The cognitive model proposes that each person's beliefs and schemas are ideographic and that two primary criteria can be used to evaluate each person's general adaptation. The first criterion is the extent to which the belief or schema is veridical; does it *correspond* to external reality or at least to the social consensus version of reality? To the extent that the person's beliefs about the world are consistent with reality, it could be argued that the person has a healthy belief system. If there is a discrepancy between beliefs and reality, the person is dysfunctional or unhealthy. The second criterion is related to *coherence*. Do the beliefs and schemas of the individual function in a coordinated manner or do some function in a discordant manner with other beliefs or schemas? To the extent that the person's beliefs are consistent with each other, it could be argued that the person is healthy. Dysfunction and disorder are marked by opposing or discordant schemas and beliefs. By implication, one of the longer term goals of cognitive therapy is to help the patient in developing both accurate and coordinated belief systems to minimize distress and maximize adaptive functioning.

Cognitive theory holds that beliefs and schemas emerge and then evolve over the course of a lifetime. They are based on individual experiences through interactions with parents, peer group influences, media effects, music and cultural experiences, unique life experiences, and traumatic experiences. Some of the common beliefs and schemas are socially shared, and these populate our cultural role and sense of self. For example, the belief in the importance of being loved is almost universal, and even though each person has his or her unique way of experiencing this felt need, it is consistent across cultures and throughout history. Certain disorders tend to run in families, and it has been proposed that this tendency results in part from the effects of parental socialization processes on their children. Thus, for example, anxious parents like their children to also be anxious, and it has been observed that the children of depressed mothers in particular are themselves at increased risk of depression (Garber & Martin, 2002; Hammen, Shih, & Brennan, 2004). On the other hand, some experiences are personal and individual and therefore provide unique characteristics of a given person's way of thinking and being in the world.

As schemas and beliefs evolve, they become self-organizing or "auto-poietic" (Guidano & Liotti, 1983; M. J. Mahoney, 1991). For example, a strong early tendency toward submission, based on living with an aggressive and sometimes violent parent, may become a superordinate self-construct that shapes the development of other social dynamics in children. As a submission schema develops, the child will likely select the types of social and other events he or she will enter, and the schema will become more elaborated and developed over time. Furthermore, once a belief or schema is in place, the experience of novel events is modified to be more consistent with the schema and may be completely accurate (Guidano & Liotti, 1983; R. E. Ingram, Miranda, & Segal, 1999). Thus, schemas may guide the attention to and perception of various aspects of the environment, just as they may affect the remembrance of past events (Strauman & Higgins, 1993). Schemas guide the emotional processing of various experiences in a manner that is increasingly consistent with the schema.

Several key phases are involved in the development of the sense of self (Guidano, 1991). Early childhood experiences are critical in the development of basic self-perceptions such as being loved or even being lovable. Basic security and attachment processes are also critical during this stage of development. Adolescence is another key period, when adolescents and young adults refine their fundamental adultlike sense of social identity and characteristic ways of thinking about and interacting with other people. In some respects, the social self emerges in adolescence and early adulthood. Gender differentiation in disorders begins to occur in this time of life. For example, adolescent girls begin to develop higher rates of anxiety disorders and depressive disorders than their male counterparts and, at least in the Western world, are more likely to develop eating disorders. In contrast, adolescent boys are more likely to develop externalizing types of disorders, including increased rates of aggression and substance abuse. It has been argued that these differential patterns of psychopathology are reflections of the cognitive organization of the self in relation to others and that the overarching patterns of cognitive organization directly affect the expression of various types of psychopathology (Guidano & Liotti, 1983; M. J. Mahoney, 1991).

In addition to the socialization and gender effects just discussed, characteristic relational patterns are associated with certain beliefs or schemas. The work of Young and colleagues is perhaps the best-elaborated cognitive model of schema organization. Young, Klosko, and Weishaar (2003) proposed that 16 schemas (referred to as *early maladaptive schemas*) may develop early in life. The schemas are organized into relational patterns, and each one has an associated set of maintenance behaviors (actions that serve to directly reinforce or strengthen schemas), compensatory behaviors (actions that may look contrary to the schema but actually serve to maintain it by virtue of the failure associated with the compensatory strategies), and avoidance behaviors (actions taken to avoid the activation of known schemas).

Other models of schema organization are worth noting. For example, Rasmussen's (2005) model of cognitive–behavioral therapy was developed on the basis of personality styles related to the system of personality dynamics and disorders in the *Diagnostic and Statistical Manual of Mental Disorders (DSM*; American Psychiatric Association, 2000). Schema models for a number of specific disorders have been developed or are in development (Riso, du Toit, Stein, & Young, 2007). Novel assessment and intervention strategies for different types of beliefs and schemas are also being developed and tested.

In practice, cognitive therapists use information from a combination of sources to develop case conceptualizations. The sources include research on the normative schemas associated with the various disorders the patient may experience, schema models such as that proposed by Young and colleagues, and the characteristics of each case. Furthermore, as the case develops and as the therapist learns more about the patient, the case conceptualization becomes more elaborate. Cognitive therapists are mindful in the development of the case conceptualization that they should look for information that not only confirms their emergent ideas in regard to the beliefs and the schemas used by the patient but also is inconsistent with their growing conceptualization. Disconfirmatory information, in particular, can provide important data that will dictate the reconceptualization of the patient's belief system.

Therapists who are learning about cognitive therapy are sometimes confused about the relationships among the various constructs that are part of the model. By way of clarification, the term *schema* is from cognitive psychology, where it was first used to refer to an organized information system (Bartlett, 1932) that might guide information processing and memory processes in any particular domain of information. Jean Piaget (1954, 1971) used the concept in his developmental model of how children learn and organize their experiences in the world. In psychopathology, the term is used primarily to refer to social information, or aspects of the self in relationship to other people. People also have emotional schemas, which are the ways in which they characteristically think about and organize information related to emotional experience. The word *belief*, which also relates to a general or characteristic way of thinking about a particular domain or set of information, is more commonly used. The term is perhaps most associated with the work of Albert Ellis, who referred to rational and irrational beliefs, which were associated with adaptive or maladaptive functioning, respectively (Ellis, 1977; Ellis & Whitely, 1979).

A term sometimes used in association with schemas and beliefs is *assumption*. An assumption reflects a propositional set of ideas, often stated in if–then form. For example, a man might assume that if he is always pleasant toward others, they will in turn treat him in a respectful and pleasant manner. Another patient might believe that if she always pleases others, then she will not be criticized. Sometimes, assumptions are also referred to as conditional assumptions to reflect the conditional nature of the proposition. Assumptions are most often directly connected to a schema or belief, and a natural correspondence exists between the beliefs that a person holds and the conditional assumptions he or she has with regard to contingencies in the world.

I believe that all of the above terms can be used more or less interchangeably. Thus, although schemas are at the core of the cognitive framework, they can be verbalized in the form of beliefs. Conditional assumptions are derived from beliefs and schemas, and they operationalize beliefs and schemas in the form of contingencies or relationships among behavior and its outcomes. All three of these concepts reflect ongoing trait-like aspects of the self. Thus, a cognitive therapist can choose the terminology and frame-

trait = habitual patterns of thought, behavior and emotion

work that best meets the needs of his or her particular patient, rather than being overly committed to any of these concepts.

Schema Assessment

Schemas can be assessed by using a number of methods. In addition to the deduction of schemas through the ongoing review of the automatic thoughts that are elicited in different situations, schemas can be evaluated through more formalized methods. One commonly employed method is the downward arrow technique, which was discussed earlier in this chapter. This technique can be used early or late in therapy both to help develop a case formulation and to evaluate a formulation that has already emerged. It can be used to examine the direct meaning attached to a particular thought or to fully explore the broader implications of a thought down to the deepest level. It can also be applied to events that the patient has experienced and to hypothetical events to see how the patient predicts he or she might respond.

In addition to clinical deduction and the downward arrow technique, other techniques can be used. As the therapist and patient start to name a schema and to consider its operation, they can engage in education and reading. Therapists could describe different schemas, for example, to see what the patients think might best fit themselves. If patients concur, therapists can assign readings about different beliefs and assumptions. This may help patients to determine which assumptions or schemas are operating in their lives. I sometimes have patients read *Reinventing Your Life* (Young & Klosko, 1994) because it describes common schemas and provides case illustrations. The popular book *Feeling Good* (Burns, 1980) provides good descriptions of a number of depression-related schemas or beliefs and how they can be effectively changed over the course of therapy. Therapists may know of a novel or book that describes a schema relevant to the patient and could be assigned as homework. For example, *The Elegance of the Hedgehog* (Barbery, 2008/2006) is a novel that includes an excellent description of a woman who lives as a spectator in relative seclusion and isolation, who through her interactions discovers that she can find deeper meaning in life through interpersonal connection and the potential for hurt and suffering that relationships involve.

Another method of assessing core schemas is through the use of questionnaires. Several questionnaires to assess beliefs or schemas related to cognitive therapy are available: the Dysfunctional Attitudes Scale (Olinger, Kuiper, & Shaw, 1987; Sahin & Sahin, 1992; A. Weissman & Beck, 1978), the Sociotropy–Autonomy Scale (A. T. Beck, Epstein, Harrison, & Emery, 1983; Bieling & Alden, 2001; Bieling, Beck, & Brown, 2000), and the Schema Questionnaire (Lee et al., 1999; Schmidt, Joiner, Young, & Telch, 1995; Welburn, Coristine, Dagg, Pontefract, & Jordan, 2002). Each of the scales has its particular domains, although the first two are more general and are designed to provide only information related to interpersonal dependencies or sociotropy and the need for independence or autonomy. The Schema Questionnaire provides scores on 16 personality dimensions, which are conceptually related to Young's schema theory. Each of the questionnaires has been evaluated in a series of studies, and the general psychometric properties of these questionnaires are sound.

Cognitive therapists need to consider when to assess schemas formally by using questionnaires. If the assessment is done too early in therapy, the patient's emotional distress may affect his or her scores. If the questionnaires are used too late, it may be difficult to get a true reading of the patient's functional belief or schemas because the patient may be out of distress or actively trying to resist thinking about his or her previous problems (Leahy, 2001). One recommendation is to use the questionnaires at the midpoint of therapy, when the therapist is beginning to formalize or is becoming clearer about the core beliefs that operate for a given patient. The patient's distress is still present and accessible enough to affect the schema questionnaire, and results of the assessment can be integrated into the case conceptualization. In my experience, questionnaires are particularly helpful if the core beliefs or schemas of the patient are confusing, complex, or conflicting among themselves. In such cases, the use of a questionnaire can significantly advance the case conceptualization. Furthermore, a discussion of the results of the questionnaire with the patient will improve the patient's understanding of the case conceptualization and will provide further information about the accuracy of the questionnaire results.

As stated previously, a general principle of cognitive therapy is that the patient and therapist work together. The process of collaborative empiricism also applies to the development of the case conceptualization. Indeed, it is good practice for the therapist to describe the general concepts of beliefs and schemas to the patient and how they operate in general. From this discussion, a more specific presentation of the critical beliefs and schemas that are critical to the patient's case conceptualization can ensue. If indicated, the therapist and patient can design behavioral homework to clarify the ways in which the patient's beliefs affect how he or she interprets situations and the emotional reactions that result from these interpretations. The cognitive therapist and patient should develop a shared case conceptualization before any efforts are made to intervene at the level of beliefs or schemas.

Ethics of Schema Change

Before the interventions for schema change are described, a few words about the ethics of schema change are in order. By definition, beliefs and schemas are pervasive; they affect all aspects of cognition, emotion, and behavior. They affect both the memories that people create of their past and the possibilities that they envision for themselves. Beliefs and schemas also influence the relationships that individuals choose for themselves and the ways in which the relationships are interpreted.

Given the omnipresent and insidious nature of beliefs and schemas, changes in them can (indeed should) have profound implications for the life of the affected person. Furthermore, the modification of the core beliefs and schemas is hard work. Such change will often involve increases in emotional distress; some sense of dysregulation; and potentially the felt need for patients to repair, modify, or change their living circumstances, employment, or social relationships (Leahy, 2001; Young et al., 2003). A respectful approach to this work, therefore, is to fully discuss the potential implications of schema change with the patient before such work is conducted. As a result of this discussion, some patients may realize the scope of change required or the implications of schema change for their social relationships and will choose not to follow the therapy through to its logical completion. For some patients, examination of the implications of schema change will increase the desire for that change. The therapist also should be mindful of the potential ramifications of schema change for other people in the patient's social world. Although the patient is the primary responsibility of the therapist, the therapist should be aware that other vulnerable people might be affected by decisions that are made in the course of therapy.

The therapist needs to respect the decisions made by the patient and follow his or her lead in terms of whether to pursue schema change. In my experience, many patients look over the "precipice" of schema change and choose not to make the leap and follow it through to its conclusion because of the perceived riskiness of the consequences. In such cases, the therapist can respectfully accept this decision, discuss the implications of avoiding schema change, consolidate the gains that have already been made, and offer the general opinion that without schema change problems may relapse or recur. After this discussion, the therapist can move toward ending the therapeutic relationship, and if possible, keep the therapeutic door open to further work, if and when the patient is ready.

Schema Interventions

Predicated on the assumption that the therapist and the patient have developed a joint conceptualization and that both agree that the schema change is indicated, there are a number of strategies for proceeding. In this section, some of the major methodologies are described, although the full range of schema change methods is likely as broad as the creativity of the therapist and the patient. Other sources to which interested readers may refer list schema change methods (J. S. Beck, 2005; D. J. G. Dobson & Dobson, 2009; Leahy, 2001, 2003; Riso et al., 2007; Young et al., 2003).

A common place to begin with schema change is the generation of a desired alternative to the current problematic belief or schema. This exploration can include discussion about such issues as the attitudes or assumptions that the new schema would entail, implied changes in behavior, interpersonal relationships, or occupations and lifestyles. Exploration of the emotional consequences of the new schema is also needed so that the patient can fully imagine the effects that are implied. One idea is to have the patient write down the different effects on his or her life that the new schema might entail. Beyond written descriptions of the new schema, imaginal techniques can sometimes help to flesh out potential operations and outcomes of the new schema.

Another technique for schema change is to identify the current maladaptive or dysfunctional schema and contrast it with the alternative that is under consideration. A range of alternative schemas may be identified to allow more flexible thinking about different ways of functioning. Consideration of different schemas also allows the therapist the opportunity to explore the patient's perspective on these alternatives. Depending on the degree of schema change that is contemplated, the therapist and patient may agree to work together to achieve these changes. In other cases, the therapist and patient may begin the process of schema change, but the patient has some distance to go to achieve his or her goals, even after the end of the formal treatment. Therapist and patient should discuss how far they will go in working together, how much change is needed before treatment ends, and the extent to which the patient and therapist are comfortable with ending treatment before complete schema change is accomplished. Even though the therapist and patient agree that further changes are warranted, external factors may limit the amount of change that is possible at the moment. In such cases, it may be possible to take a therapeutic holiday and to resume schema change work at a later point in time.

The patient should view alternative schemas as realistic and achievable over some definite time period. If the alternatives are seen as incredible or unachievable, the motivation to change will often lag. Schema change can be pursued in stages, just as successive approximation is used in behavioral and automatic thought work. Once the viable alternative schema has been identified, it should be fleshed out. Therapists may include questions about the attitudes that would be associated with a schema change and differences among current patterns of relationships and those that would be indicated by the new schema. Perhaps new activities, occupations, relationships, or lifestyles need to be discussed. Any concerns expressed by the patient or an inability to imagine new schemas in operation during this elaboration may warn the therapist that the change is too great or that the patient is experiencing anxiety about the change being discussed. Techniques that can be used by the therapist to explore the new schema include imagery, parables, or stories to demonstrate how different people adapt to varying life circumstances. The reading of biographies and novels may also be helpful. A useful homework assignment might be to have the patient talk with friends or family about the kind of change that he or she is considering. Such discussions can provide alternative vantage points that the patient can use in considering the advantages and disadvantages of as well as the prospects for change. Furthermore, responses of other people in the patient's social circle can help him or her to evaluate the amount of social or interpersonal "push back" that might be experienced if he or she starts to make changes. Since the goal of schema change is the development of a stable new way of being in the world, a supportive social environment is a critical factor.

A formal way to evaluate the existing and proposed schemas is with the use of a pros-and-cons chart listing advantages and disadvantages of schema change. Four quadrants are established for each of the old and new schemas: the advantages versus disadvantages and the short- versus long-term perspectives. The setup is exemplified in Figure 4.7. Although patients tend only to focus on the advantages of schema change, the pros–cons matrix forces the therapist and patient to explore more fully the disadvantages of schema change and the advantages of maintaining the current negative schema.

Examination of the advantages of the current negative schema or the disadvantages of a new and likely more adaptive schema may at first seem counterintuitive. However, these issues must be considered as part of the process of schema change because the patient will almost certainly do this work by himself or herself. For example, common disadvantages of schema change can include disequilibrium or confusion in social relationships, anxiety about enacting new schemas, and social disruption. Often what therapists experience as resistance to change is actually the natural and healthy way that people protect themselves from anxiety and threat

Old schema: *My work defines my worth.*

Time Perspective	Advantages	Disadvantages
Short term		
Long term		

New schema: *My work is important, but it does not define my worth.*

Time perspective	Advantages	Disadvantages
Short term		
Long term		

Figure 4.7

Pros-and-cons worksheet for schema change.

(Leahy, 2001), and such reactions should be anticipated when a schema change is attempted. On the other side of the chart, a common advantage of maintaining the existing negative schema is that it is more "comfortable" for the patient; even though it may cause certain forms of distress, it involves known processes, and the patient will experience relatively little confusion in his or her social roles if the old schema is maintained. Sometimes the exploration of the short- and long-term advantages and disadvantages of the old and new schema will lead to a reevaluation of the new schema and the amount of turmoil it may cause. In such cases, an alternative new schema may be developed during therapy, and the process of examining the pros and cons of change can be repeated.

As with automatic thoughts, evidence-based strategies can be used to promote schema change. The data log is commonly used if the therapist believes that the patient already has life experiences that are consistent with the new schema being developed but is not paying attention to the experience. The data log has two blocks of space (see Figure 4.8) for recording experiences that might be consistent with the new schema or inconsistent with the old schema. The patient is also asked to pay attention to experiences that might be more consistent with or supportive of the old schema and to try reinterpreting the experiences either to minimize their effect or to see them as consistent with the new schema. The data log can also be used in conjunction with homework assignments, in which the patient purposely tries to act in a manner consistent with the

Old schema: *No one loves me.*

New schema: *If I treat myself as lovable, others will come to like or love me.*

Data that are consistent with the old schema, but with reinterpretation:
Data that are consistent with the new schema or inconsistent with the old schema:

Figure 4.8

Data log method.

new schema. This can be helpful to the patient in seeing the types of reactions generated in the social environment and whether the experiences are consistent with the new schema. If this homework strategy is used, the therapist must review the evidence to ensure that the patient interprets his or her experience as consistent with the new schema.

Public declaration is another technique for the promotion of schema change. Once the patient is ready, he or she speaks with important other people in his or her life and makes a commitment to change. The commitment can be relatively simple, such as "I have always lived my life as if I am second best, but I'm going to try to treat myself better from now on." It can be more elaborate and include a long discussion about the desired changes that the patient wants to create or detailed descriptions of the proposed new self. These declarations ideally are made in person, but patients also can write detailed descriptions of the changes they want to make and present them to important people in their lives as preludes to discussion. This technique is helpful in the identification of social supports for intended change as well as of people who may present resistance to intended change.

Another technique that can be used to promote schema change is the personal eulogy. In this technique, patients write the type of eulogy that they would want to have read at their funeral. This technique, perhaps somewhat morbid, encourages patients to look forward and imagine the type of person that they would like to be remembered as. This exercise can be kept private or can be shared with other people.

Behavioral enactment is perhaps the single most potent technique for schema change. Also referred to as the "as if" technique, this strategy involves the patient actually acting in a manner consistent with the new schema as a way to explore the schema and its effects. In a sense, this strategy is like trying on a new overcoat to see how it feels and to observe the reactions of other people. If the developmental work that involved imagining the new schema has been thorough and the patient is fully committed to trying out the new schema, this technique will provide powerful information about its advantages and disadvantages. If this technique is used, the therapist must fully evaluate how the experiment felt to the patient in the subsequent session. Equally important is evaluation of the reactions of others to the patient, although the patient will need to be encouraged to keep clear the distinction between his or her experience of the technique and the reactions of others.

When the as if technique is used, the patient should be prepared for the range of interpersonal reactions that might occur. For example, people in the patient's life may provide considerable negative feedback for the intended changes, and as a result the patient may experience distress and doubt about the course of action that he or she has chosen. Preparation for negative outcomes is paramount in enabling the patient to learn from the experience and not simply view it as a failure. At the other extreme, the patient may discover a new and different way to live and idealize or over-react to the experience. As with other aspects of cognitive therapy, therapists and patients should explore both the advantages and disadvantages of any changes that are observed.

Another technique that can promote schema change, especially as related to past experiences, is confrontation and exploration. The technique can vary dramatically in terms of content and scope. For example, it can involve something as basic as thinking about the past and the developmental experiences associated with negative schemas. A historical review can help the patient to determine key experiences and people who were involved in the development of dysfunctional schemas. Perusing photograph albums and visiting areas of personal historic significance are more dramatic ways of evoking emotional memories.

A riskier form of confrontation and exploration involves the patient talking with other people who were present during key developmental phases in his or her life to explore from the others' perspectives what occurred and how the patient responded to the events. In its most dramatic form, this strategy can include direct confrontation of people in the patient's life, in particular, the people who were associated with negative developmental experiences. For example, a patient could confront his mother about the negative parenting practices that led to beliefs or schemas that subsequently caused problems in his life. A female adolescent might confront her father about a pattern of verbal or physical abuse that he meted out to her as a child. Obviously, the use of confrontation or exploration needs to be carefully considered, and both the advantages and the disadvantages of the technique should be fully explored before the technique is attempted.

Acceptance and Cognitive Therapy

After the patient has explored the advantages and disadvantages of schema change, or in some other cases, has attempted a degree of schema change, he or she might decide that further schema change is either unwarranted or too difficult. In such cases, a strategic shift toward acceptance of negative schemas can be used as an alternative technique. This generally involves recognition of the negative schema and exploration of its developmental origins, and therapist and patient reach an agreement that a schema change at that point in the patient's life is not feasible. The cognitive model proposes that if negative schemas are maintained, the patient will remain vulnerable to further disorder and distress, and this should be discussed. On the other hand, the patient has the right to accept or refuse schema change. If the patient decides that further schema change is not possible, the therapist should respect the decision.

Strategies for acceptance include learning how to cope with difficult people or situations, learning how to better tolerate emotional distress, and recognizing the early signs of relapse or recurrence of the problems that brought the patient into therapy. Coping strategies can be promoted so that the patient can better accept the likely ongoing distress he or she will feel. They could include relaxation, escape from the situation, deescalation of conflict techniques, or cognitive reinterpretation to reduce the negative effects of interpersonal difficulties. These coping strategies are essentially efforts to limit the negative effects of ongoing core beliefs.

The development of resiliency and positive coping is an alternative approach to limiting ongoing distress. The patient could be encouraged to develop resources or interests that are not directly connected to the schema but that could promote a sense of autonomy and the ability to cope should negative experiences occur. For example, patients could be encouraged to develop new and supportive social activities or interests, or they could be encouraged to try initiatives that provide a sense of social support.

Mindfulness and meditation have recently been adapted as cognitive therapy techniques (Kuyken et al., 2008; Segal, Williams, & Teasdale, 2002; Williams, Teasdale, Segal, & Kabat-Zinn, 2007). This development is similar in many respects to the integration of ideas related to mindfulness and acceptance of negative experience seen in other areas of psychotherapy (Germer, Siegel, & Fulton, 2005) and particularly in cognitive–behavioral therapy (Baer, 2006; Hayes, Follette, & Linehan, 2004; Hayes, Strosahl, & Wilson, 1999). The development of the ability to be aware of negative experiences and to simply observe them as part of the passing events of life can significantly reduce the likelihood that the patient will make further negative appraisals of negative experience. A formal course in meditation may teach patients how to observe experiences without reacting negatively to them. Mindfulness strategies are also being used to prevent relapse in some disorders (Ma & Teasdale, 2004).

ENDING THERAPY

How much cognitive therapy is enough? When is it appropriate to end therapy? These questions do not have a ready answer. Although in some cases it is relatively clear when the patient's treatment goals have been met and he or she is ready for treatment to end, in many cases it is not. More frequently, patients come to therapy with a series of problems or goals. Some of them are fully addressed during therapy, some are partially addressed, and some may be named or identified but not really changed at all. Psychotherapy can be likened to standing in a stream: The therapist enters the patient's "life stream" for a period of time, tries to change things that are going on around him or her, but then steps out of the water while the stream continues to flow. In this section, the ways in which cognitive therapists think about ending therapy are discussed, and strategies to facilitate the end of therapy are provided.

Given that many patients do not fully achieve their treatment goals, one of the critical questions is when to move to end the treatment program. As noted in a previous chapter, cognitive therapists typically endorse the ongoing assessment of treatment outcomes and the renegotiation of treatment goals as the case conceptualization develops and treatment evolves (J. S. Beck, 1995; Persons, 2008). If the primary treatment goals have been fully or largely attained, the cognitive therapist will likely begin to discuss the idea of ending treatment with the patient. The patient may be happy to have this discussion, especially if the goals have been attained. In other cases, the patient may be reluctant to end the treatment. In such cases, the costs and benefits of either ending treatment or continuing it for a particular period of time should be discussed. This discussion signals to the patient that even issues such as termination are open for discussion and that cognitive therapy is a collaborative process. However, the therapist is not bound to continue treatment past the point when he or she thinks that it is indicated simply because the patient is nervous about ending treatment or perhaps has developed a dependency on the therapy. The therapist retains the responsibility of deciding when treatment is no longer indicated and of making a referral or simply ending treatment, as is clinically appropriate.

A full exploration of the implications of ending therapy includes examination of the feelings of both the patient and the therapist with regard to this action. Often the patient will become anxious when he or she considers the end of treatment, as this transition signals the loss of a major social support. If the treatment has gone well, the patient often feels a sense of pride in his or her relationship with the therapist, and the therapist may have become a major confidant. Therapists need to be sensitive to these patient reactions and to explore them respectfully, even if the decision is to end therapy. Likewise, the therapist is ideally able to express his or her reactions until the end of therapy, to congratulate the patient on the successes that he or she has made, to commiserate about ongoing problems in the patient's life, and to offer support by either providing a referral or future treatment if the patient's condition should change.

To some extent, the end of psychotherapy is envisioned as soon as it begins. In the context of cognitive therapy, which is time limited and problem oriented, the temporary nature of the therapy relationship is explicit. Indeed, most therapy cases begin with a decision about which problem or problems will be addressed and the establishment of a timeline in which to conduct the treatment. The cognitive therapist will from time to time remind the patient about the number of sessions that have been held and how many are likely to remain. If the originally projected treatment limit is reached, the therapist and patient will renegotiate the issue, with an eye to the remaining problems and the amount of time needed to address them.

Cognitive therapy is also an educational therapy. Patients are taught the methods of cognitive therapy for their long-term use. Patients are trained in the techniques that are used, in the language of cognitive therapy, in planning for termination, and in becoming as self-sufficient as possible in the conduct of therapy. The use of forms and procedural guidelines helps to communicate the general structure of therapy to the patient. A common experience is that the patient learns the major methods that have been helpful over the course of treatment and in a sense masters these skills. Cognitive therapists will often give the patient the tools that were used in treatment (blank forms, written assignments, or other documentation). The therapist and patient may have used a self-help manual during treatment, and of course this is part of the tool set that the patient takes away at the end of treatment. An implicit goal in cognitive therapy is for the patient to develop a sense of self-efficacy and competence with respect to the management of ongoing or emergent issues.

One of the techniques that I have used to assist in the process of ending therapy is a therapy notebook. The notebook can consist of a scribbler or book with either blank or lined pages, but it is essentially a document that the patient begins at the beginning of therapy, develops over the course of treatment, and takes away when treatment ends. The notebook can include the activity schedules, a list of major homework assignments, automatic thought records, schema-based treatment ideas, or a list of the major things that the patient has learned over the course of therapy. In many respects, it is a chronicle of the therapy process, and it can be used by the patient after the end of formal therapy to review the treatment strategies that were helpful or to design new homework without the therapist being present.

Another strategy that is often used to help the patient to move toward the end of treatment is the fading of treatment sessions. Fading is a process whereby the patient and therapist agree to skip a week or two between therapy sessions so that the patient can practice the techniques and can learn how to cope more independently with life difficulties. The process is most effective when the major treatment goals of cognitive therapy have been met but the patient faces continuing issues or dilemmas. Fading often helps the patient to build a sense of self-efficacy and can reduce the anxiety that he or she may otherwise feel about the end of treatment.

A method that can be used in conjunction with fading is the self-session. This method consists of the patient sitting down alone and proceeding through the typical steps of a cognitive therapy session. Thus, he or she can determine recent issues that need to be evaluated, set an agenda to consider these issues, use the techniques that have been learned over the course of cognitive therapy, and assign himself or herself a homework task. Self-sessions are particularly helpful in the period between therapy sessions as therapist and patient move toward the end of active treatment. A benefit of the self-session is in determining where the patient tends to become stuck or has difficulties in thinking through alternative ways of dealing with ongoing problems. These issues can be discussed in the next therapy session and can provide an opportunity for discussing areas for continued work.

When the end of treatment is imminent, a common strategy in cognitive therapy is to ask the patient to prepare for it with a series of questions. The questions can be asked of the patient verbally or can be assigned as written homework to be brought to one of the last treatment sessions. The precise nature of the questions that will be posed to any given patient will vary, but in general can include some of the questions presented in Figure 4.9. They could be used as a written homework assignment in anticipation of the final therapy session.

Cognitive therapy ends when the patient and therapist agree that the major treatment goals have been met and that the patient has the tools or the skills to work with ongoing issues that may arise. Cognitive therapists often use their case formulation in considering when to end therapy and may share it with the patient, so that both the therapist and the patient feel that the major issues have been addressed. Furthermore, if a set of intake questionnaires was completed when treatment began, cognitive therapists often will assess the patient with the same set to verify that significant change has occurred. Again, the results are typically shared with the patient

Complete the following questions before the last session of therapy. Bring this form to the session to discuss with your therapist.

1. What were the major problems you addressed in therapy?
2. What remaining problems or issues do you face?
3. What skills have you learned in cognitive therapy that helped you?
4. What problems do you anticipate will occur in the future?
5. How will you use your skills to address remaining or future problems?
6. How confident are you that you can solve your ongoing problems?
7. How do you feel about the end of treatment?
8. Do you have a plan if you find that your symptoms return or that you cannot cope with your problems?
9. Write down here the phone number of your cognitive therapist or other resources you might need in the future:

Figure 4.9

Questions to ask at the end of cognitive therapy.

so that he or she can appreciate how much change has occurred, what symptoms remain, and what vulnerabilities for future distress might be present.

Therapy may end before all of the treatment goals have been met. Unfortunately, even with the best efforts of the therapist and the patient, the treatment may be ineffective. In this case, it is appropriate for the therapist to review the case conceptualization with the patient, to conduct a final assessment of functioning and symptomatology, and to offer a referral for alternative care. This follow-up evaluation will help both the patient and the therapist to understand the remaining difficulties and likely will improve the quality of a referral, if this outcome is indicated.

RELAPSE PREVENTION

Cognitive therapists generally believe that difficulties emerge as beliefs or schemas in concert with life stresses. All individuals have unique vulnerabilities, and everyone can suffer distress, depression, or other difficulties under certain circumstances. Almost by definition, people who have already been in therapy have identifiable vulnerabilities, and such people can be expected to have increased risk for problems relative to the population at large. Indeed, one of the greatest risk indicators for a number of disorders is a history of that same problem (Antony et al., 2005). As part of the overall review of treatment and termination assessment, cognitive therapists will share their understanding of what remaining vulnerabilities exist for each patient and may make predictions about what types of stressors might lead to future difficulties. Together, the therapist and patient can anticipate problems and plan how to manage them if they occur. The therapist will generally encourage the use of cognitive therapy techniques and principles appropriate for the particular problems that are anticipated.

If the patient is likely to experience a recurrence of symptoms or to encounter a life situation that he or she might not be able to cope with, the cognitive therapist should make himself or herself available to help before the problems manifest as more extreme or serious symptoms or disorders. A quick return to therapy for a focused and brief period may be indicated. Some cognitive therapists, if they anticipate that the patient is likely to struggle in the future, might arrange for a follow-up appointment at some definite time after the end of treatment. The appointment can be used to assess any symptomatology the patient is experiencing, to assess how he or she is coping with any current problems, to anticipate future problems, to reinforce the use of cognitive therapy procedures, and to help with any other issues that may have arisen. In either instance, the use of a small number of booster sessions, especially at a critical point in time, can help to consolidate the lessons learned in cognitive therapy and to reduce the likelihood of relapse or the recurrence of psychopathology. In the context of depression, this strategy to reduce the likelihood of relapse has been likened to the process of seeing a dentist for preventive dental care (Bieling & Antony, 2003).

The research on preventive aspects of cognitive therapy has not kept pace with research on the use of cognitive therapy in the acute treatment of disorders. Although this relative lack of research on the costs and benefits of preventive therapy is regrettable, it is understandable from the perspective that most health care systems focus on the remediation and treatment of acute symptoms and problems in large measure because this is where patients also place their focus. It is hoped that more efforts will be made in prevention science in the coming years to learn when and how cognitive therapy procedures are maximally effective and efficient.

5

Evaluation

This chapter addresses issues of importance in the field of cognitive therapy. One is the evidence base for cognitive therapy, which is one of the strongest among all of the various schools of psychotherapy (Cook, Biyanova, & Coyne, 2009; Epp & Dobson, 2010; Messer, 2004). The strength of evidence has been cited as a factor in the promotion of cognitive therapy globally and in the dissemination of its methods in graduate programs in psychology and psychiatry (Cook et al., 2009; M. M. Weissman et al., 2006). The second issue addressed relates to the conceptual limits of the model and the conceptual and empirical areas that remain for development. Although cognitive therapy has been well developed and evaluated in a number of areas, research questions and problems remain, which are briefly discussed in this chapter. Finally, the issues of training and dissemination are touched on. Since the treatment approach has strong evidence to support it, effective means for the training and credentialing of therapists are important issues for consideration.

EVIDENCE BASE FOR COGNITIVE THERAPY

The evidence base to support cognitive therapy is particularly strong in certain clinical domains (Epp & Dobson, 2010). Cognitive therapy is the treatment of choice for many of the anxiety disorders. Cognitive therapy is an effective treatment method for patients with depression, with results that are similar to those of pharmacotherapy in the acute phase of treatment and superior to pharmacotherapy over the longer term (Hollon, 1996, 2003; Strunk & DeRubeis, 2001). In the area of bulimia nervosa, cognitive therapy is the most effective psychotherapy to date and should be considered the treatment of choice (Shapiro et al., 2007; Whittal, Agras, & Gould, 1999).

Table 5.1 summarizes the evidence for cognitive therapy and related cognitive–behavioral therapies (CBTs). As can be seen in the table, CBT has absolute efficacy (i.e., evidence of success relative to no treatment or treatment as usual) for many psychological disorders. It demonstrates treatment equivalence with or superiority to pharmacotherapy and other psychotherapy for many other conditions. In addition to anxiety and depression, cognitive therapy enjoys considerable success in substance abuse disorders, personality disorders, pain, somatoform disorder, couple problems, and others. The evidence database continues to grow, and new treatments are being developed every year. With so many ongoing trials in cognitive therapy, it has become difficult to stay current with outcome research.

Although the overall results are consistent and provide excellent data in support of cognitive therapy and CBT, a few caveats to the general conclusion exist. First, CBT has not been tested as a stand-alone treatment for some conditions. For example, cognitive therapy is almost always tested as an adjunct to pharmacotherapy in bipolar disorder, and an aspect of CBT in the treatment of bipolar disorder is medication adherence. In the area of psychosis, CBT also is largely used in an adjunctive role because pharmacotherapy remains the predominant treatment. Second, literature reviews often fail to distinguish adequately among CBTs. As noted above, cognitive therapy is just one of the broader psychotherapies in the CBT family. Given the lack of distinctions made in the outcome literature, whether the tenets of cognitive therapy per se are essential for successful

Table 5.1

Summary of Efficacy Findings by Disorder or Problem

Disorder	Treatment	Absolute efficacy	Efficacy relative to medications	Efficacy relative to other psychotherapies
Unipolar depression	CBT	+	+	≈
Bipolar disorder*	CBT	+		=
Specific phobia	Exposure and cognitive restructuring	++	+	+
Social phobia	Exposure and cognitive restructuring	++	≈	≈
Obsessive–compulsive disorder	Exposure and response prevention and cognitive restructuring	+		+
Panic disorder	Exposure and cognitive restructuring	++	≈	+
Chronic post–traumatic stress disorder	Exposure and cognitive techniques	+		=
Generalized anxiety disorder	CBT	+	+	+
Bulimia nervosa	CBT	+	+	+
Binge eating disorder	CBT	+		=
Anorexia nervosa	CBT	+	+	=
Schizophrenia*	CBT	+		+

(continued)

Table 5.1
Summary of Efficacy Findings by Disorder or Problem (*Continued*)

Disorder	Treatment	Absolute efficacy	Efficacy relative to medications	Efficacy relative to other psychotherapies
Marital distress	CBT	+		≈
Anger and violent offending	CBT	+		
Sexual offending	CBT	+	−**	+
Chronic pain	CBT	+		
Borderline personality disorder	CBT	+		≈
Substance use disorders	CBT	+		≈
Somatoform disorders	CBT	+	+	=
Sleep difficulties	CBT	+	+	+

Note. A blank space indicates insufficient or no evidence; − indicates negative evidence; + indicates positive evidence; = indicates approximate equivalence; ++ indicates treatment of choice; ≈ indicates equivocal evidence; "CBT" indicates efficacy of specific components unknown; * indicates that CBT (cognitive–behavioral therapy) is typically used as an adjunct to medication in these disorders; ** indicates efficacy relative to physical treatments (i.e., surgical castration and hormonal treatments). From *Handbook of Cognitive–Behavioral Therapies* (3rd ed., p. 60), by K. S. Dobson, 2010, New York, NY: Guilford Press. Copyright 2010 by Guilford Press. Reprinted with permission.

treatment outcome or whether a more generic CBT is needed is unclear. Third, as is often noted in literature reviews, the quality of individual psychotherapy studies is variable, and the number of studies done in different areas also varies. Thus, the quality or strength of the evidence base is different for different practice areas. A careful practitioner will want to know the evidence base in his or her practice area before interpreting the literature to his or her patients.

One of the difficulties associated with the growth of cognitive therapy is that a number of the treatments emphasize various aspects of the cognitive model. For example, while cognitive theory posits a key role for schematic processes and the role of negative automatic thoughts, some treatments place greater emphasis on behavior change and commensurately less on cognitive work. Although the cognitive model of psychopathology is often invoked in these treatments, the interventions do not necessarily follow the techniques that are listed in this book. Recently, there has also been a shift away from theory-based interventions to the development of transdiagnostic models of intervention (Barlow, Allen, & Choate, 2004). This approach emphasizes that different interventions may work well across disorders (Ellard, Fairholme, Boisseau, Farchione, & Barlow, 2010), whereas many cognitive therapy manuals suggest the need for a case conceptualization that is driven by diagnostic considerations. Ultimately, the research literature must evaluate the tenets of cognitive therapy, the need for the various interventions that are embedded in the approach (Gortner, Gollan, Dobson, & Jacobson, 1998; Jacobson et al., 1996), and the clinical utility of alternative models of treatment, including the transdiagnostic approach.

REMAINING QUESTIONS

Some of the important issues that remain with respect to the development of cognitive therapy are identified in this section, including limits of the cognitive model and the clinical problems of relapse and recurrence. Two difficulties that are derived from the success of the approach—cultural adaptation and sensitivity—and the strategies for dissemination and training are also discussed.

Limits of the Model

Cognitive therapy presents a particular model of psychopathology and treatment and is included in the broader class of psychotherapies referred to as the cognitive–behavioral therapies (K. S. Dobson, 2010). Some of the other treatment methods within this broader class include rational emotive behavior therapy, problem-solving therapy, and stress inoculation therapy. A frequent question in this field concerns the similarities and differences between cognitive therapy and CBT. Unfortunately, no definitive clarification of the boundary between these therapies can be made. The former tends to emphasize the schematic and core belief issues that underlie specific problems and symptoms, whereas CBT is somewhat broader in its focus on current adaptive functioning and development. Both approaches include cognitive and behavioral aspects in their conceptualization of problems and in their treatment technology. In some respects, cognitive therapy has "become" the field of CBT, since it dominates many of the conceptual and treatment developments. The distinction between the approaches may become a matter of linguistics rather than a practical reality.

Failure, Relapse, and Recurrence

Even while cognitive therapy enjoys considerable outcome success, one of the difficulties of the approach is the limits of its efficacy. The success rates for some anxiety disorders can reach as high as 90% (i.e., 90% of patients who complete treatment will lose their anxiety disorder diagnosis), but the success rates for other disorders are considerably lower (Epp & Dobson, 2010). Furthermore, the success rates are for patients who complete treatment; dropout is a problem in a number of treatment areas. Finally, while there is evidence that cognitive therapy reduces the likelihood of relapse in some areas, actual rates of relapse and recurrence suggest that further work is needed in modifying risk factors.

The above problems are not unique to cognitive therapy. They speak to the heterogeneity of mental disorders and the probability that any one conceptual model might not account for the expression of different disorders. A wide range of biological, psychosocial, and social risk factors have been identified for many disorders (e.g., K. S. Dobson & Dozois, 2008), and cognitive therapy probably does not adequately address all of these risk factors. Whether cognitive theory can evolve and incorporate other elements of the theory to account for the risk for various disorders more fully and whether such theoretical and treatment expansion leads to more comprehensive treatments with higher success rates or lower relapse rates remain to be seen. In the short term, the relatively high rates of treatment failure and relapse and recurrence for various disorders speak to the need for ongoing theory development, treatment expansion, and clinical trials.

Sociocultural Adaptations and Diversity Considerations

The relative success of cognitive therapy among the various schools of psychotherapy carries with it several risks. For example, the approach may be developed in one cultural context but applied to other cultures in an indiscriminate fashion. Within a specific society, a treatment technique may be developed for work with adults but applied to children in a way that may not be developmentally appropriate. Similarly, treatments developed in a predominantly female (or male) sample may not work with the other gender. A treatment model or technique may be developed for one clinical condition but applied to others without proper consideration or evaluation. All of these issues are examples of how well cognitive therapy generalizes from one culture, group, or condition to another. From another perspective, the ability to get similar results in various groups speaks to the robustness or generalizability of cognitive theory and therapy.

Humans vary dramatically in many dimensions, including age, gender, mental and physical well-being or challenges, sexual orientation and behavior, social and cultural history and experience, linguistic heritage, socioeconomic status, and more. Cognitive theory and therapy methods are most often developed in one particular context or for one particular group. Thus, it is critical that the tenets and outcomes of theory and therapy be evaluated with regard to their sociocultural appropriateness, acceptability, and efficacy when applied to other groups (Duckworth,

2009; Martell, Safren, & Prince, 2004; Pantalone, Iwamasa, & Martell, 2010; Reinecke & Simmons, 2005). The remarkable explosion of the cognitive and CBTs around the world signals that these approaches likely have considerable generalizability and can be applied broadly. However, the extent to which cultural or any other diversity consideration might limit success needs to be explored systematically. In this way, cultural or other adaptations to cognitive therapy can be made so that the approach is maximally effective wherever it is used.

Training and Dissemination

Cognitive therapists generally accept the idea that treatments need to be written in manualized form (Chambless & Ollendick, 2001; Luborsky & DeRubeis, 1984) so that therapists who learn the approach can determine whether they are applying it appropriately. Treatment manuals also provide the opportunity for psychotherapy researchers to state with confidence that the treatments that were investigated were applied appropriately, that the necessary treatment components were included, and that extraneous or theoretically inconsistent methods or techniques were excluded. In principle, when a treatment manual is evaluated, the field can have confidence that the approach is being appropriately applied and that the conclusions about the efficacy of that specific treatment are sound.

Psychotherapy techniques are disseminated less systematically than are psychotherapy research results (Addis, 1997). Therapists adopt a given treatment approach for a variety of reasons: it may have been the model that their graduate training program provided, they may have had the opportunity to obtain training because of where they live, a specific book or manual may have been written in or translated into their language, workshops may have emerged from time to time, and so on. The training in psychotherapy tends to be somewhat happenstance, and it is often a matter of opportunity or desire. Furthermore, most mental health practitioners and therapists are evaluated for their training and competence at the time that they obtain a license to practice, but they do not typically require ongoing evaluation of psychotherapy competence, even if they expand the scope of their training or services. Some therapists may claim competence in various forms of psychotherapy despite having had limited exposure or training and possibly no supervision in the approaches they claim competence in. Even if supplemented with training, treatment manuals may not be the best form of dissemination (Addis, 1997; Sholomskas et al., 2005).

Given the relative lack of control over training but the relatively high status of cognitive therapy due to its treatment efficacy, it is not surprising that some therapists claim competence in this approach despite having received no formal training and no supervision. The fidelity of these therapists to cognitive therapy, both from the perspective of adherence to the specific features of the treatment and the competence with which the various techniques are applied, is a matter that should be openly questioned. On the other hand, there is no gold standard training program or model for developing competency in cognitive therapy. Most training programs incorporate a combination of didactic instruction, directed readings, treatment experience, and either individual or group supervision. How much training in these various dimensions is required, what type of supervised experience is optimal, what specific readings should be incorporated into the training, and so on, are questions that have no definitive answer.

In partial response to the question of how to best disseminate cognitive therapy, different groups have begun to elucidate credentialing standards. The British Association of Behavioural and Cognitive Psychotherapies (BABCP; http://www.babcp.com/) has a training curriculum that incorporates core training and supervised experience in the practice of CBT. The BABCP accredits practitioners, supervisors and trainers, and training courses. This approach emphasizes the "input" or training variables required to attain mastery in the field, including the course work and supervision aspects.

In contrast with the BABCP, the Academy of Cognitive Therapy (ACT; http://www.academyofct.org/) has developed a credentialing process that focuses on the "output" or performance variables associated with successful cognitive therapy. Thus, while applicants for the status of Diplomate in Cognitive Therapy have to attest to basic instruction and reading in the field, the process emphasizes the ability to conduct a case conceptualization from a cognitive therapy perspective and the successful conduct of a psychotherapy session as rated by experts (K. S. Dobson, Beck, & Beck, 2005).

Which of the two above approaches is the more appropriate one for developing competence in cognitive therapy? We do not know at present. Indeed, training in the field of psychotherapy is still conducted much as it was when psychotherapy began, and evaluation of the efficacy and effectiveness of different dissemination strategies is only beginning (Sholomskas et al., 2005). Until the field develops standardized assessment strategies for the evaluation of successful training, psychotherapy training will likely also stay in a relatively undeveloped state. The evaluation of training for cognitive therapy probably will need to have two components, one related to case conceptualization and the other to actual in-session therapy behavior. The credentialing system of ACT is likely the closest that exists for a comprehensive evaluation of competence to practice cognitive therapy.

6

Future Developments

Although cognitive therapy has come a long distance from its beginnings, and many more clinical applications are in use than existed 40 years ago, much remains to be done. The concepts of cognitive theory, research evaluations of cognitive models of psychopathology, tools and technologies for theory evaluation, and consideration of aspects of psychopathology that cut across disorders continue to develop. The conceptual underpinnings will lead to advances in the treatment methods for a wide range of disorders, including some that were thought to be relatively untreatable from a cognitive therapy perspective.

The methodologies of psychotherapy research and the statistical tools used to measure outcomes continue to evolve. The diagnostic formulation and assessment of disorders continue to evolve as well, and these innovations are advancing the psychotherapy research literature. New cognitive and hybrid treatment models are being developed and written into manuals, and these manuals are being subjected to careful outcome evaluation. Other professionals are evaluating the strategies for the training and dissemination of cognitive therapy and cognitive–behavioral therapy (CBT) and are providing evidence about how to deliver treatments that have been shown to be effective in clinical trials. Recent work has been undertaken to connect the outcome assessment and training/dissemination work with policy development and funding for effective psychotherapies (D. M. Clark et al., 2009; McHugh & Barlow, 2010). Although this work is not specific to cognitive therapy (nor should it be), the evidence related to cognitive therapy and CBT has placed it at the forefront of policy consideration, funding, and dissemination efforts.

Cognitive therapy clearly has become the prominent approach to psychotherapy in the early part of the 21st century (K. S. Dobson & Dozois, 2010). In the Western world, patients and consumer groups are beginning to advocate for the development and delivery of evidence-based treatments, including cognitive therapy. The first 40 years in the development of cognitive theory and therapy have led to almost meteoric growth, and it will be interesting to see what the next 40 years hold. At the end of the day, the goals of cognitive theory and therapy are to understand patient distress and disorder and to provide the most effective and efficient treatments. With this social imperative in mind, cognitive therapy has much to recommend it.

7

Summary

Cognitive therapy is without a doubt one of the most successful of the psychotherapies. This success can be observed in terms of the established influence and evidence base for this approach to psychotherapy.

One of the features of cognitive therapy is that it rests on a cognitive model of psychopathology, a model broad and generic enough that other disorders can be conceptualized from this perspective. The cognitive therapy model may have begun in the area of clinical depression, but it was quickly adapted to anxiety disorders, relational problems, personality disorders, anger, and psychosis, among others.

Given its time-limited and symptom-focused nature, cognitive therapy also fits well within the movement toward evidence-based practice, or what have been called *empirically supported therapies* in the context of psychotherapy. Another factor that has assisted with development of cognitive therapy, and empirically supported therapies more generally, has been the development of diagnostic systems.

HISTORY

Attendant to the incorporation of cognitive processes in models of behavior change, the late 1970s saw the emergence of cognitive and behavioral therapy methods, or what was called at that time cognitive-behavior modification.

Into the above set of paradigmatic changes came what many saw as an outstanding research result. In a National Institute of Mental Health-funded clinical research trial, which directly contrasted the efficacy of cognitive therapy for depression against a well-established antidepressant medication, the two therapies were reported to have equal outcomes. Furthermore, the 1-year follow-up results yielded a nonsignificant advantage in favor of cognitive therapy. These results were received with great enthusiasm in the emerging world of cognitive–behavioral therapy (CBT), but with great skepticism in the psychiatric world.

CBT grew out of behavior therapy and social learning theory but has expanded dramatically over the years to include a variety of models and approaches. The field of CBT includes cognitive therapy, rational emotive behavior therapy, stress inoculation training, self-instructional training, problem-solving therapy, dialectical behavior therapy, and acceptance and commitment therapy, among others.

THEORY

In contrast to the *information processing model* of cognition, as reflected in the constructs of structure, process, content, and product, a model of cognition was formulated specifically in the context of cognitive therapy. According to the *cognitive model* of cognition, individuals possess cognitive structures, which are a composite of both formal (semantic) and personal (autobiographical or episodic) knowledge and experience. Various terms have been used to refer to these structures, but the most common terms are *beliefs* and *schemas*. Within the cognitive model, schemas are seen as both *reactive,* in that they respond to and incorporate new information, and *proactive,* in that they influence which types of situations a person might be willing to enter, the information that is attended to in different situations or contexts, and even the range of experiences an individual is able to have.

Key schemas have been found for depression. Many authors have identified key schemas in other disorders: anxiety disorders, anger problems, panic disorder, insomnia, and anorexia nervosa, among them. Models either have been or are being developed for a wide range of other disorders and clinical problems, including personality disorders.

Cognitive models can be specific to disorders, but schemas may also follow common patterns that cut across disorders. In 1983, Aaron Beck and colleagues identified the two schema themes of sociotropy and autonomy to reflect this idea and developed the Sociotropy–Autonomy Scale to measure these constructs. From this perspective, sociotropy reflects an interpersonal dependency and the personal belief that one needs interpersonal relations and support to function. Sociotropic persons are vulnerable to anxiety if their interpersonal relationships are threatened or to depression if these relationships are actually disrupted or broken. In contrast, autonomous persons tend to define themselves in terms of their individual achievements, accomplishments, and degree of independence/autonomy. Autonomous persons become anxious if their autonomy is threatened and depressed if they suffer a blow to their sense of achievement or accomplishment. As can be seen, these constructs are not specific to a particular disorder but cut across different emotional response patterns.

One of the more difficult assumptions related to the schema model is that schemas lie relatively dormant until primed or activated by a relevant situation or trigger. So, for example, a person who has a strong interpersonal dependency schema will function well and appear to be functionally independent unless his or her interpersonal relationships are threatened, at which time negative thoughts, emotions, and behaviors might all be demonstrated. The assumption of "silent schemas" has been expressed as a diathesis–stress process, in that schemas represent a diathesis or vulnerability to distress or dysfunctional behavior, but only when activated by a relevant stressor.

Once a schema is activated by a trigger or situation, the cognitive model holds that the information that the individual is experiencing is appraised. Appraisals can be benign or potentially positive, depending on the nature of the event and the corresponding schemas. Most of the focus in cognitive therapy, however, is on more insidious and negative appraisals. Beck and colleagues have argued that in psychopathology, negative appraisals tend to be reflexive and automatic, as they reflect overlearned reactions to various types of situations. Although these appraisals or *automatic thoughts* are often made without conscious effort or deliberation, they can be brought to awareness and evaluated with appropriate training and skills.

The concept of automatic thoughts actually encompasses different aspects of the information processing model of cognition. The actual thoughts are the product of information processing, which includes attention to the trigger or stimulus situation, thoughts about the situation (e.g., rumination, distorted appraisals), appraisals of the meaning of the situation as mediated by the schemas, and the production of a cognitive product, which is the thought itself. Cognitive theorists have elucidated a variety of possible ways that situations can be misperceived or distorted to yield negative outcomes. These cognitive distortions are selectively used by patients in ways that help to maintain the integrity and stability of schemas, even sometimes at the risk of the emotional health of the patient.

Cognitive models have been criticized for giving "primacy" to cognitive processes and relegating emotions and behaviors to consideration as epiphenomenal experience. In contrast, it has been argued that certain experiences are sensory or emotional in nature and do not require cognitive processing. There is now considerable research in the domain of "effortful" and "automatic" information processing. Furthermore, recent descriptions of cognitive therapy tend to recognize the reciprocal influences of cognition, emotion, behavior, and the environment more than did earlier descriptions, which tended to be more linear. Cognitive mediation of situations and events is a principal assumption of the cognitive model of psychopathology, and this assumption is reflected in the key interventions of cognitive therapy. Although cognitive therapists will at times use more behavioral or directly emotive therapy techniques, the majority of the methods rely on cognitive mediation, reinterpretation, or both mediation and reinterpretation for their effect.

The cognitive model proposes that schemas are based on developmental experiences, which can include early interactions with parents, early exposure to different types of living environments, and different social interactions. Schemas are also based on messages that are received from the world at large, such as television, radio, or print media. As children grow and develop their own social circles, these relationships also exert an influence on schema development and maintenance.

If schemas are in some cases problematic, why do they develop? There are two general processes by which children develop schemas that become problems for them later in life. One is that the parents are themselves disturbed in some way and inadvertently engage in behaviors that cause schema problems in their children. The second possibility is that whereas the bases of schemas develop primarily in childhood, when the child is dependent on others for sustenance and care, schemas survive into adulthood, when the person is responsible for his or her own care.

THE THERAPY PROCESS

Most patients come to treatment with a set of problems, and an initial stage of cognitive therapy is helping them to name, differentiate, and evaluate the extent of these problems. The cognitive therapist and the patient will work to solve these problems or to minimize their negative effects. A substantial amount of time in cognitive therapy is spent in teaching new skills that can be used to undermine existing problems.

However, the model also notes that core schemas form part of the basis of the development of problems. Schema change can undermine problems, or at least the perception that a current social situation is problematic. Indeed, a number of the interventions in cognitive therapy promote schema change.

Cognitive therapy is a complex form of psychotherapy. It rests on a particular patient–therapist relationship, and this relationship is considered to be a necessary but not sufficient aspect of the treatment. The techniques of cognitive therapy include aspects of problem identification and problem solving, cognitive and behavioral skills training, and schema identification and modification. Which specific techniques are used with which patient, in what order, and with what outcomes is predicated on an individualized case assessment and conceptualization. The ability to form a therapeutic relationship, to assess and conceptualize diverse cases and to select and apply the broad range of possible techniques takes time, training, supervision, and practice.

Cognitive therapy rests on several key principles: the focus on current adaptation and present problems, time-limited treatment, structured therapy, the key roles of activity and homework, a focus on the therapeutic relationship, collaborative empiricism, psychoeducation, technical eclecticism, and treatment as prevention. A corollary of some of these principles is that cognitive therapists try not only to treat the present problems but also to reduce the likelihood of their recurrence and to develop skill sets in their patients to respond to any such recurrence. Thus, the use of a case formulation that rests on the cognitive model provides a certain structure for understanding each case, and this formulation can be communicated to the patient for reuse after therapy. Moreover, since the treatment addresses underlying schemas, which represent vulnerability or risk factors for dysfunction, successful cognitive therapy should reduce the likelihood of future problems.

The beginning steps with patients in cognitive therapy include the potential use of questionnaires or other test instruments, an intake interview, the development of a preliminary case conceptualization, a discussion with the patient about the appropriateness of the approach for him or her, a discussion of treatment goals, and the development of a preliminary contract for therapy. Ideally, what emerges from these beginning steps is an initial agreement between the therapist and patient about the problem or problems that will be targeted in therapy, a preliminary case conceptualization that is based on both general cognitive models and the specifics of the case, a beginning positive relationship that can develop over the course of time, and an initial general plan.

Many people consider the interventions with automatic thoughts to be the hallmarks of cognitive therapy. Indeed, there are many strategies to work with negative thinking, and not all of them are described in this volume.

Various methods can be used to collect information about automatic thoughts. If the thought is relatively simple and repetitive, recording its frequency might be sufficient. In such cases a golf counter can be used to collect frequency information. The thought can be monitored and may become less frequent as it is challenged over the course of therapy. The dysfunctional thought record (DTR) was initially developed to assess the automatic thoughts of depressed patients; however, the DTR is generally useful in conducting the assessment of automatic thoughts across a range of problems.

Once the patient begins to notice and record the automatic thoughts that occur in different situations, the therapist encourages the patient to bring them into treatment. The therapist needs to support this activity because sometimes simply exposing the thoughts is difficult for the patient. Once automatic thoughts are being consistently reported in treatment, appropriate interventions can be selected. Three broad classes of interventions for negative automatic thoughts can be distinguished by the manner in which the patient might answer the following three questions:

1. What evidence supports or does not support the automatic thought?
2. What are the viable alternative thoughts in this situation?
3. What meaning is attached to the automatic thought?

Evidence-Based Interventions for Automatic Thoughts

In general, the first set of interventions that a cognitive therapist will consider relates to the match or mismatch between the automatic thought and the situation or trigger. A common kind of distortion is negative fortune-telling, or predicting a negative outcome in a certain circumstance. Another common type of cognitive distortion is negative attribution. Negative attributions occur regularly in depression: Patients often blame themselves for perceived failure. Labeling is yet another type of cognitive distortion that lends itself to an evidence-based intervention. People engage in labeling as a shorthand way to describe themselves or others. Labels are often extreme and almost by definition are categorical. When the cognitive therapist hears a patient engaging in the process of labeling, he or she can undertake a series of interventions.

Alternative-Based Interventions

The second class of interventions in working with negative thoughts is the examination of alternatives. In some cases, a review of the evidence related to a negative automatic thought indicates that the original thought is not justified. In such instances, the patient can be asked for a more reasonable and accurate rendition of the situation.

A more formal strategy for encouraging alternative responses to negative automatic thoughts is a technique called the *rational role-play*. In this technique, the therapist asks the patient to state his or her automatic thoughts. Another strategy for examining reasonable alternatives to negative automatic thoughts involves homework. In this type of exercise, the patient is encouraged to identify *possible* alternative thoughts, even in the absence of evidence and even if the alternatives do not seem credible. The use of humor is another strategy for generating alternative perspectives to negative thoughts. Jokes and humor often require a sudden shift in perspective.

Another technique for encouraging alternative thoughts is to ask the patient how useful or adaptive the original negative thought was. *Emotional reasoning* is a type of negative thought that lends itself well to an examination of alternatives. Emotional reasoning occurs when people use their emotional response to a situation to justify the automatic thought that led to the response.

Developing Positive Thoughts

The interventions described here have focused on the identification and reduction of negative thoughts. Cognitive therapists also encourage the development of positive thoughts.

Meaning-Based Interventions

The third class of interventions used in working with automatic thoughts is the examination of the meanings attached to or the inferences that are drawn from different experiences. Often, the inferences are themselves automatic thoughts, which are about either other thoughts or the emotional and behavioral consequences of these thoughts. When a cognitive therapist asks the patient questions about the meanings or inferences that have been drawn from automatic thoughts, the discussion often moves from situation-specific thinking to more general and trait-like patterns of thought. The technique known as the *downward arrow* has been well-documented. Rather than disputing or challenging negative thoughts, the therapist asks the patient to assume that the first automatic thought is true or valid, then further queries the patient about the inference or conclusion that he or she has drawn. The therapist's question can also be described as the "So what?" question, as in "So what if your thought is true? What would that mean about you?"

Working With Core Beliefs and Schemas

Cognitive psychology has provided key information about the processes by which individuals develop functional or dysfunctional beliefs and schemas. Clinical cognitive psychopathology combines a broad theoretical framework with the ideographic processes that have led to the individual patient's distress and problems in adaptive coping. Schemas can be assessed by using a number of methods. In addition to the deduction of schemas through the ongoing review of the automatic thoughts that are elicited in different situations, schemas can be evaluated through more formalized methods. One commonly employed method is the above-mentioned downward arrow technique.

By definition, beliefs and schemas are pervasive; they affect all aspects of cognition, emotion, and behavior. They affect both the memories that people create of their past and the future possibilities that they envision for themselves. Beliefs and schemas also influence the relationships that individuals choose for themselves and the ways in which those relationships are interpreted. Once the therapist and the patient have developed a joint conceptualization and have agreed that schema change is indicated, a number of strategies can be applied.

After the patient has explored the advantages and disadvantages of schema change or has attempted a degree of schema change, he or she might decide that further schema change is unwarranted or too difficult. In such cases, a strategic shift toward acceptance of negative schemas can be used as an alternative technique. This generally involves recognition of the negative schema, exploration of its developmental origins, and an agreement between the therapist and the patient that a schema change at that point in the patient's life is not feasible.

In some cases it is clear when the patient's treatment goals have been met and the patient is ready for treatment to end, but in many cases it is not. Frequently, patients come to therapy with a series of problems or goals. Some of them are fully addressed during therapy, some are partially addressed, and some may be named or identified but not really changed at all. The ways in which cognitive therapists think about ending therapy are discussed, and strategies to facilitate the end of therapy are provided.

Cognitive therapists generally believe that difficulties emerge as beliefs or schemas in concert with life stresses. All individuals have unique vulnerabilities, and everyone can suffer distress, depression, or other difficulties under certain circumstances. Almost by definition, people who have already been in therapy have identifiable vulnerabilities, and such people can be expected to have increased risk for problems relative to the population at large. Indeed, one of the greatest risk indicators for a number of disorders is a history of that same problem. As part of the overall review of treatment and termination assessment, cognitive therapists will share their understanding of what remaining vulnerabilities exist for each patient and may make some predictions about what types of stressors might lead to future difficulties.

EVALUATION

Some of the important issues that remain with respect to the development of cognitive therapy are identified, including potential limits of the cognitive model and the clinical problems of relapse and recurrence.

The relative success of cognitive therapy among the various schools of psychotherapy carries with it several risks. For example, the approach may be developed in one cultural context but applied in other cultures in an indiscriminate fashion. Within a specific society, a treatment technique may be developed for work with adults but applied to children in a way that may not be developmentally appropriate. Similarly, treatments developed in a predominantly female (or male) sample may not work with the other gender. A treatment model or technique may be developed for one clinical condition but applied to others without proper consideration or evaluation.

Cognitive therapists generally accept the idea that treatments need to be written in a manualized form so that therapists who learn the approach determine whether they are applying it appropriately. Treatment manuals also provide the opportunity for psychotherapy researchers to state with confidence that the treatments that were investigated were applied appropriately, that the necessary treatment components were included, and that extraneous or theoretically inconsistent methods or techniques were excluded. In principle, when a treatment manual is evaluated, the field can have confidence that the approach is being appropriately applied and that the conclusions about the efficacy of that specific treatment are sound.

FUTURE DEVELOPMENTS

Although cognitive therapy has come a long distance from its early beginnings and many more clinical applications are in use than existed 40 years ago, much remains to be done. The concepts of cognitive theory, research evaluations of cognitive models of psychopathology, tools and technologies for theory evaluation, and consideration of aspects of psychopathology that cut across disorders continue to develop. The conceptual underpinnings will lead to advances in the treatment methods for a wide range of disorders, including some that were thought to be untreatable from a cognitive therapy perspective.

Glossary of Key Terms

ASSUMPTION   A propositional set of ideas, often stated in if–then form. Assumptions are directly connected to a schema or belief, and a correspondence exists between the beliefs that a person holds and the conditional assumptions he or she has with regard to contingencies in the world.

AUTOMATIC THOUGHT   A thought that occurs in a specific situation or context and that is the product of information processing. Automatic thoughts include attention to the trigger or stimulus situation, thoughts about the situation (e.g., rumination, distorted appraisals), and appraisals of the meaning of the situation as mediated by the schemas.

BELIEF   The term *belief* is largely synonymous with *schema*. A general or characteristic way of thinking about a particular domain or set of information.

CASE CONCEPTUALIZATION   The description of the mechanisms that the patient uses to create and maintain his or her problems. Cognitive case conceptualizations include a description of core beliefs or schemas, assumptions, triggers or activating events for schemas, automatic thoughts, and the resulting cognitive/behavioral/emotional processes. Case conceptualization is a core process in cognitive therapy and guides the treatment plan and interventions that are used.

COGNITIVE MODEL OF PSYCHOPATHOLOGY   A system that considers symptoms and problems from the information processing model of cognition and concepts such as beliefs and schemas, assumptions, automatic thoughts, and their emotional and behavioral consequences.

COGNITIVE–BEHAVIORAL THERAPY   A broad set of psychotherapies that includes cognitive therapy, rational emotive behavior therapy, stress inoculation training, self-instructional training, problem-solving therapy, dialectical behavior therapy, and acceptance and commitment therapy, among others. Cognitive–behavioral therapies emphasize the development of adaptive thinking and behavior to overcome mental and physical disorders.

COGNITIVE THERAPY   A system of psychotherapy that is part of the broader set of cognitive–behavioral therapies. Cognitive therapy, which is associated with its creator, Aaron Beck, rests on a cognitive model of disorder and case conceptualization and uses a broad range of techniques to change core beliefs and situation-specific thinking and behavior.

COLLABORATIVE EMPIRICISM   The idea that the therapist and patient work together as a team to identify problems, areas of needed change, and optimal ways to effect change in the patient's life. Collaborative empiricism is guided by the notions of evidence and objectivism.

CONSTRUCTIVISM   In contrast to realism, constructivism holds that the existence of an objective, external reality is either wrong or a weak and untestable premise. From a constructivist perspective, human adjustment is not defined by the correspondence between perception and the real world but in the coherence or integrity of experience.

DOWNWARD ARROW   An efficient method of exposing core beliefs, which begins with the identification of a negative automatic thought and proceeds to examine the implications of the thought or the inferences drawn until a broad underlying belief is identified.

HOMEWORK   The assignments, tasks, missions, or experiments conducted by the patient between one therapy session and the next.

INFORMATION PROCESSING MODEL   A systematic perspective about the human cognitive system and the manner in which information is apprehended and processed. This model includes constructs such as cognitive structures, content, processes, and products.

REALISM   In contrast to constructivism, realism proposes that events occur in the real world, regardless of whether someone perceives their occurrence and whether they are perceived accurately. From this epistemological perspective, human adjustment is reflected by optimal accuracy in perception of the world.

SCHEMA   Adapted from cognitive psychology, the concept refers to an organized system that guides information processing and memory processes. In addition to schemas for the material world, schema content in cognitive therapy includes self-schemas, schemas for interpersonal relationships, and emotional schemas.

Suggested Readings

Antony, M. M., Ledley, R., & Heimberg, R. G. (Eds.). (2005). *Improving outcomes and preventing relapse in cognitive–behavioral therapy*. New York, NY: Guilford Press.

Bennett-Levy, J., Butler, G., Fennell, M., Hackmann, A., Meuller, M., & Westbrook, D. (Eds.). (2004). *Oxford guide to behavioural experiments in cognitive therapy*. Oxford, England: Oxford University Press.

Bond, F. W., & Dryden, W. (Eds.). (2004). *Handbook of brief cognitive behaviour therapy*. New York, NY: Wiley.

Dobson, D. J. G., & Dobson, K. S. (2009). *Evidence-based practice of cognitive–behavior therapy*. New York, NY: Guilford Press.

Dobson, K. S. (Ed.). (2010). *Handbook of cognitive–behavioral therapies* (3rd ed.). New York, NY: Guilford Press.

Freeman, A. (Ed.). (2005). *Encyclopedia of cognitive behavior therapy*. New York, NY: Plenum Press.

Freeman, A., Pretzer, J., Fleming, B., & Simon, K. M. (2004). *Clinical applications of cognitive therapy* (2nd ed.). New York, NY: Kluwer Academic/Plenum.

Gilbert, P. (Ed.). (2004). *Evolutionary theory and cognitive therapy*. New York, NY: Springer.

Gilbert, P., & Leahy, R. L. (2007). *The therapeutic relationship in the cognitive behavioral psychotherapies*. New York, NY: Routledge.

Hays, P., & Iwamasa, G. (Eds.). (2006). *Culturally responsive cognitive–behavioral therapy: Assessment, practice, and supervision.* Washington, DC: American Psychological Association.

Kazantzis, N., Deane, F., Ronan, K., & L'Abate, L. (Eds.). (2005). *Using homework assignments in cognitive–behavioral therapy.* New York, NY: Routledge.

Leahy, R. L. (2003). *Cognitive therapy techniques: A practitioner's guide.* New York, NY: Guilford Press.

Leahy, R. L. (Ed.). (2003). *Roadblocks in cognitive-behavioral therapy: Transforming challenges into opportunities for change.* New York, NY: Guilford Press.

Leahy, R. L. (Ed.). (2004). *Contemporary cognitive therapy: Theory, research, and practice.* New York, NY: Guilford Press.

Leahy, R. L., & Dowd, T. E. (Eds.). (2002). *Clinical advances in cognitive psychotherapy: Theory and application.* New York, NY: Springer.

Ledley, D. R., Marx, P., & Heimberg, R. G. (2005). *Making cognitive–behavioral therapy work: Clinical process for new practitioners.* New York, NY: Guilford Press.

Lyddon, W. J., & Jones, J. V. (Eds.). (2001). *Empirically supported cognitive therapies: Current and future applications.* New York, NY: Springer.

Neenan, M., & Dryden, W. (2000). *Essential cognitive therapy.* London, England: Whurr.

Neenan, M., & Dryden, W. (2004). *Cognitive therapy: 100 key points and techniques.* New York, NY: Routledge.

O'Donohue, W., Fisher, J., & Hayes, S. (2004). *Cognitive behavior therapy: Applying empirically supported techniques in your practice.* New York, NY: Wiley.

Persons, J. B. (2008). *The case formulation approach to cognitive–behavior therapy.* New York, NY: Guilford Press.

Reinecke, M., & Clark, D. (Eds.). (2003). *Cognitive therapy across the lifespan: Evidence and practice.* Cambridge, England: Cambridge University Press.

Schuyler, D. (2003). *Cognitive therapy: A practical guide.* New York, NY: Norton.

Simos, G. (Ed.). (2002). *Cognitive behaviour therapy: A guide for the practicing clinician.* New York, NY: Brunner-Routledge.

Wells, A. (2002). *Emotional disorders and metacognition: Innovative cognitive therapy.* New York, NY: Wiley.

Wright, J. H, Basco, M. R., & Thase, M. E. (2005). *Learning cognitive–behavior therapy: An illustrated guide.* Arlington, VA: American Psychiatric Publishing.

References

Addis, M. E. (1997). Evaluating the treatment manual as a means of disseminating empirically validated psychotherapies. *Clinical Psychology: Science and Practice, 4*(1), 1–11. doi:10.1111/j.1468-2850.1997.tb00094.x

Alford, B. A., & Beck, A. T. (1997). *The integrative power of cognitive therapy.* New York, NY: Guilford Press.

American Psychiatric Association. (2000). *Diagnostic and statistical manual of mental disorders* (4th ed., text rev.). Washington, DC: American Psychiatric Association Press.

American Psychological Association. (2006). Evidence-based practice in psychology. *American Psychologist, 61,* 271–285. doi:10.1037/0003-066X.61. 4.271

Antony, M. M., Ledley, D. R., & Heimberg, R. G. (Eds.). (2005). *Improving outcomes and preventing relapse in cognitive–behavioral therapy.* New York, NY: Guilford Press.

Antony, M. M., & Swinson, R. P. (2000). *Phobic disorders and panic in adults: A guide to assessment and treatment.* Washington, DC: American Psychological Association. doi:10.1037/10348-000

Arnkoff, D. (1980). Psychotherapy from the perspective of cognitive theory. In J. M. Mahoney (Ed.), *Psychotherapy process: Current issues and future directions* (pp. 339–361). New York, NY: Plenum Press.

Arnkoff, D. (1986). A comparison of the coping and restructuring components of cognitive restructuring. *Cognitive Therapy and Research, 10,* 147–158. doi:10.1007/BF01173721

Baer, R. A. (Ed.). (2006). *Mindfulness-based treatment approaches: Clinician's guide to evidence base and applications.* San Diego, CA: Academic Press.

Bandura, A. (1977). *Social learning theory.* Englewood Cliffs, NJ: Prentice-Hall.

Bandura, A. (1986). *Social foundations of thought and action: A social cognitive theory.* Englewood Cliffs, NJ: Prentice-Hall.

Barbery, M. (2008/2006). *The elegance of the hedgehog* (A. Anderson, Trans.). New York, NY: Europa Editions.

Barlow, D. H. (1996). Health care policy, psychotherapy research, and the future of psychotherapy. *American Psychologist, 51,* 1050–1058. doi:10.1037/0003-066X.51.10.1050

Barlow, D. H., Allen, L. B., & Choate, M. I. (2004). Toward a unified treatment for emotional disorders. *Behavior Therapy, 35,* 205–230. doi:10.1016/S0005-7894(04)80036-4

Bartlett, F. C. (1932). *Remembering.* Cambridge, England: Cambridge University Press.

Beck, A. T. (1988). *Love is never enough.* New York, NY: Harper & Row.

Beck, A. T. (1999). *Prisoners of hate: The cognitive basis of anger, hostility, and violence.* New York, NY: HarperCollins.

Beck, A. T., & Emery, G. (1985). *Anxiety disorders and phobias: A cognitive perspective.* New York, NY: Basic Books.

Beck, A. T., Epstein, N., Harrison, R. P., & Emery, G. (1983). *Development of the sociotropy–autonomy scale: A measure of personality factors in psychopathology. Preliminary write-up.* Philadelphia: University of Pennsylvania, Department of Psychiatry.

Beck, A. T., Freeman, A., & David, D. D. (2004). *Cognitive therapy of personality disorders* (2nd ed.). New York, NY: Guilford Press.

Beck, A. T., Rector, N. A., Stolar, N., & Grant, P. (2009). *Schizophrenia: Cogntive theory, research and therapy.* New York, NY: Guilford Press.

Beck, A. T., Rush, A. J., Shaw, B. F., & Emery, G. (1979). *Cognitive therapy of depression.* New York, NY: Guilford Press.

Beck, J. S. (1995). *Cognitive therapy: Basics and beyond.* New York, NY: Guilford Press.

Beck, J. S. (2005). *Cognitive therapy for challenging problems: What to do when the basics don't work.* New York, NY: Guilford Press.

Bieling, P. J., & Alden, L. E. (2001). Sociotropy, autonomy, and the interpersonal model of depression: An integration. *Cognitive Therapy and Research, 25,* 167–184. doi:10.1023/A:1026491108540

Bieing, P. J., & Antony, M. M. (2003). *Ending the depression cycle: A step-by-step guide for preventing relapse.* Oakland, CA: New Harbinger.

Bieling, P. J., Beck, A. T., & Brown, G. K. (2000). The Sociotropy–Autonomy Scale: Structure and implications. *Cognitive Therapy and Research, 24,* 763–780. doi:10.1023/A:1005599714224

Bieling, P. J., Beck, A. T., & Brown, G. K. (2004). Stability and change of sociotropy and autonomy subscales in cognitive therapy of depression. *Journal of Cognitive Psychotherapy, 18,* 135–148. doi:10.1891/jcop.18.2.135.65962

Bieling, P. J., & Kuyken, W. (2003). Is cognitive case formulation science or science fiction? *Clinical Psychology: Science and Practice, 10*(1), 52–69. doi:10.1093/clipsy.10.1.52

Blackburn, I. M., James, I. A., & Flitcroft, A. (2006). Case formulation in depression. In N. Tarrier (Ed.), *Case formulation in cognitive behavior therapy* (pp. 113–141). New York, NY: Routledge.

Burns, D. (1980). *Feeling good.* New York, NY: William Morrow.

Castonguay, L. G., & Beutler, L. E. (2006). *Principles of therapeutic change that work.* New York, NY: Oxford University Press.

Chambless, D. L. (1999). Empirically validated treatments—What now? *Applied & Preventive Psychology, 8,* 281–284. doi:10.1016/S0962-1849(05)80043-5

Chambless, D. L., & Hollon, S. D. (1998). Defining empirically supported therapies. *Journal of Consulting and Clinical Psychology, 66,* 7–18. doi:10.1037/0022-006X.66.1.7

Chambless, D. L., & Ollendick, T. H. (2001). Empirically supported psychological interventions: Controversies and evidence. *Annual Review of Psychology, 52,* 685–716. doi:10.1146/annurev.psych.52.1.685

Clark, D. A., Beck, A. T., & Alford, B. A. (1999). *Scientific foundations of cognitive theory and therapy of depression.* New York, NY: Wiley.

Clark, D. A., Beck, A. T., & Stewart, B. (1990). Cognitive specificity and positive–negative affectivity: Complementary or contradictory views on anxiety and depression? *Journal of Abnormal Psychology, 99,* 148–155. doi:10.1037/0021-843X.99.2.148

Clark, D. M. (1986). A cognitive model of panic. *Behaviour Research and Therapy, 24,* 461–470. doi:10.1016/0005-7967(86)90011-2

Clark, D. M., Layard, R., Smithies, R., Richard, D. A., Suckling, R., & Wright, B. (2009). Improving access to psychological therapy: Initial evaluation of two UK demonstration sites. *Behaviour Research and Therapy, 47,* 910–920. doi:10.1016/j.brat.2009.07.010

Cook, J. M., Biyanova, T., & Coyne, J. C. (2009). Influential psychotherapy figures, authors, and books: An Internet survey of over 2,000 psychotherapists.

Psychotherapy: Theory, Research, Practice, Training, 46(1), 42–51. doi:10.1037/a0015152

Coyne, J. C., & Gotlib, I. H. (1983). The role of cognition in depression: A critical appraisal. *Psychological Bulletin, 94,* 472–505. doi:10.1037/0033-2909.94.3.472

Coyne, J. C., & Whiffen, V. E. (1995). Issues in personality as diathesis for depression: The case of sociotropy-dependency and autonomy-self-criticism. *Psychological Bulletin, 118,* 358–378. doi:10.1037/0033-2909.118.3.358

Craighead, E., Sheets, E., Bjornsson, A., & Amarson, E. (2005). Specificity and nonspecificity in psychotherapy. *Clinical Psychology: Science and Practice, 12,* 189–193. doi:10.1093/clipsy.bpi024

DeRubeis, R. J., Evans, M. D., Hollon, S. D., Garvey, M. J., Grove, W. M., & Tuason, V. B. (1990). How does cognitive therapy work? Cognitive change and symptom change in cognitive therapy and pharmacotherapy for depression. *Journal of Consulting and Clinical Psychology, 58,* 862–869. doi:10.1037/0022-006X.58.6.862

Dobson, D. J. G., & Dobson, K. S. (2009). *Evidence-based practice of cognitive–behavior therapy.* New York, NY: Guilford Press.

Dobson, K. S. (Ed.). (2010). *Handbook of cognitive–behavioral therapies* (3rd ed.). New York, NY: Guilford Press.

Dobson, K. S., Beck, J. S., & Beck, A. T. (2005). The Academy of Cognitive Therapy: Purpose, history, and future prospects. *Cognitive and Behavioral Practice, 12,* 263–266. doi:10.1016/S1077-7229(05)80031-8

Dobson, K. S., & Craig, K. D. (1998). *Empirically support therapies: Best practice in professional psychology.* Thousand Oaks, CA: Sage.

Dobson, K. S., & Dozois, D. J. A. (2010). Historical and philosophical bases of the cognitive-behavioral therapies. In K. S. Dobson (Ed.), *Handbook of cognitive–behavioral therapies* (3rd ed.; pp. 3–38). New York, NY: Guilford Press.

Dobson, K. S., & Dozois, D. J. A. (Eds.). (2008). *Risk factors in depression.* San Diego, CA: Academic Press.

Dobson, K. S., & Hamilton, K. E. (2003). Cognitive restructuring: Behavioral tests of negative cognitions. In W. O'Donohue, J. E. Fisher, & S. C. Hayes (Eds.), *Empirically supported techniques of cognitive behavior therapy: A step-by-step guide for clinicians* (pp. 74–88). New York, NY: Wiley.

Duckworth, M. P. (2009). Cultural awareness and culturally competent practice. In W. O'Donohue & J. E. Fisher (Eds.), *General principles and empirically supported techniques of cognitive–behavior therapy* (pp. 63–76). New York, NY: Wiley.

D'Zurilla, T. J., & Nezu, A. M. (2007). *Problem-solving therapy: A positive approach to clinical intervention* (3rd ed.). New York, NY: Springer.

Elkin, I., Gibbons, R. D., Shea, M. T., Sotsky, S. M., Watkins, J. T., & Pilkonis, P. A. (1995). Initial severity and differential treatment outcome in the National Institute of Mental Health Treatment of Depression Collaborative Research Program. *Journal of Consulting and Clinical Psychology, 63,* 841–847. doi:10.1037/0022-006X.63.5.841

Elkin, I., Shea, M. T., Watkins, J. T., Imber, S. D., Sotsky, S. M., Collins, J. F., . . . Parloff, M. B. (1989). NIMH treatment of depression collaborative research program: I. General effectiveness of treatments. *Archives of General Psychiatry, 46,* 971–982.

Ellard, K. K., Fairholme, C. P., Boisseau, C. L., Farchione, T. J., & Barlow, D. H. (2010). Unified protocol for the transdiagnostic treatment of emotional disorders: Protocol development and initial outcome data. *Cognitive and Behavioral Practice, 17,* 88–101. doi:10.1016/j.cbpra.2009.06.002

Ellis, A. (1977). The basic clinical theory of rational-emotive therapy. In A. Ellis & R. Greiger (Eds.), *Handbook of rational-emotive therapy* (pp. 3–34). New York, NY: Springer.

Ellis, A., & Whitely, J. M. (Eds.). (1979). *The practice of rational-emotive therapy. Theoretical and empirical foundations of rational-emotive therapy.* Monterey, CA: Brooks/Cole.

Emmelkamp, P. M. G., & Aardema, A. (1999). Metacognition, specific obsessive-compulsive beliefs and obsessive-compulsive behaviour. *Clinical Psychology & Psychotherapy, 6,* 139–145. doi:10.1002/(SICI)1099-0879(199905)6:2<139::AID-CPP194>3.0.CO;2-9

Epp, A. M., & Dobson, K. S. (2010). The evidence base for cognitive–behavioral therapy. In K. S. Dobson (Ed.), *Handbook of cognitive–behavioral therapies* (3rd ed., pp. 39–74). New York, NY: Guilford Press.

Fairburn, C. G. (2008). *Cognitive behavior therapy and eating disorders.* New York, NY: Guilford Press.

Fruzzetti, A. E., & Erikson, K. R. (2010). Mindfulness and acceptance interventions in cognitive–behavioral therapy. In K. S. Dobson (Ed.), *Handbook of cognitive–behavioral therapies* (3rd ed., pp. 347–373). New York, NY: Guilford Press.

Garber, J., & Martin, N. C. (2002). Negative cognitions in offspring of depressed parents: Mechanisms of risk. In S. H. Goodman & I. H. Gotlib (Eds.), *Children of depressed parents: Mechanisms of risk and implications for treatment* (pp. 121–153). Washington, DC: American Psychological Association. doi:10.1037/10449-005

Germer, C. K., Siegel, R. D., & Fulton, R. (Eds.). (2005). *Mindfulness and psychotherapy.* New York, NY: Guilford Press.

Gortner, E. T., Gollan, J. K., Dobson, K. S., & Jacobson, N. S. (1998). Cognitive–behavioral treatment for depression: Relapse prevention. *Journal of Consulting and Clinical Psychology, 66,* 377–384. doi:10.1037/0022-006X.66.2.377

Greenberger, D., & Padesky, C. A. (1995). *Mind over mood: Change how you feel by changing the way you think.* New York, NY: Guilford Press.

Guidano, V. F. (1984). A constructivist outline of cognitive processes. In M. A. Reda & M. J. Mahoney (Eds.), *Cognitive psychotherapies: Recent developments in theory, research and practice* (pp. 31–45). Cambridge, MA: Ballinger.

Guidano, V. F. (1991). *The self in process.* New York, NY: Guilford Press.

Guidano, V. F., & Liotti, G. (1983). *Cognitive processes and emotional disorders: A structural approach to psychotherapy.* New York, NY: Guilford Press.

Hammen, C., Shih, J. H., & Brennan, P. A. (2004). Intergenerational transmission of depression: Test of an interpersonal stress model in a community sample. *Journal of Consulting and Clinical Psychology, 72,* 511–522. doi:10.1037/0022-006X.72.3.511

Hartlage, S., Alloy, L. B., Vasquez, C., & Dykman, B. (1993). Automatic and effortful processing in depression. *Psychological Bulletin, 113,* 247–278. doi:10.1037/0033-2909.113.2.247

Harvey, A. G. (2006). What about patients who can't sleep? Case formulation for insomnia. In N. Tarrier (Ed.), *Case formulation in cognitive behaviour therapy* (pp. 293–311). New York, NY: Routledge.

Hayes, S. C., Follette, V. M., & Linehan, M. M. (Eds.). (2004). *Mindfulness and acceptance: Expanding the cognitive–behavioral tradition.* New York, NY: Guilford Press.

Hayes, S. C., Strosahl, K. D., & Wilson, K. G. (1999). *Acceptance and commitment therapy: An experiential approach to behavior change.* New York, NY: Guilford Press.

Held, B. S. (1995). *Back to reality: A critique of postmodern theory in psychotherapy.* New York, NY: Norton.

Hollon, S. D. (1996). The efficacy and effectiveness of psychotherapy relative to medications. *American Psychologist, 51,* 1025–1030. doi:10.1037/0003-066X.51.10.1025

Hollon, S. D. (2003). Does cognitive therapy have an enduring effect? *Cognitive Therapy and Research, 27*(1), 71–75. doi:10.1023/A:1022538713914

Ingram, R. E., & Kendall, P. C. (1986). Cognitive clinical psychology: Implications of an information processing perspective. In R. E. Ingram (Ed.), *Information processing approaches to clinical psychology* (pp. 3–21). London, England: Academic Press.

Ingram, R. E., Miranda, J., & Segal, Z. V. (1999). *Cognitive vulnerability to depression.* New York, NY: Guilford Press.

Jacobson, N. S., Dobson, K. S., Truax, P. A., Addis, M. E., Koerner, K., Gollan, J. K., . . . Prince, S. E. (1996). A component analysis of cognitive–behavioral treatment for depression. *Journal of Consulting and Clinical Psychology, 64,* 295–304. doi:10.1037/0022-006X.64.2.295

Jacobson, N. S., & Hollon, S. D. (1996). Prospects for future comparisons between drugs and psychotherapy: Lessons from the CBT-versus-pharmacotherapy exchange. *Journal of Consulting and Clinical Psychology, 64,* 104–108. doi:10.1037/0022-006X.64.1.104

Kazantzis, N., & Deane, F. P. (1999). Psychologists' use of homework assignments in clinical practice. *Professional Psychology: Research and Practice, 30,* 581–585. doi:10.1037/0735-7028.30.6.581

Kazantzis, N., Deane, F., Ronan, K., & L'Abate, L. (Eds.). (2005). *Using homework assignments in cognitive–behavioral therapy.* New York, NY: Routledge.

Kendall, P. C., Howard, B. L., & Hays, R. C. (1989). Self-referent speech and psychopathology: The balance of positive and negative thinking. *Cognitive Therapy and Research, 13,* 583–598. doi:10.1007/BF01176069

Kendall, P. C., & Ingram, R. E. (1987). The future for cognitive assessment of anxiety: Let's get specific. In L. Michelson & L. M. Ascher (Eds.), *Anxiety and stress disorders: Cognitive–behavioral assessment and treatment* (pp. 89–104). New York, NY: Guilford Press.

Kingdon, D. G., & Turkington, D. (2005). *Cognitive therapy of schizophrenia.* New York, NY: Guilford Press.

Kiresuk, T. J., Stelmachers, Z. T., & Schultz, S. K. (1982). Quality assurance and goal attainment scaling. *Professional Psychology, 13,* 145–152. doi:10.1037/0735-7028.13.1.145

Klerman, G. L., Weissman, M. M., Rounsaville, B. J., & Chevron, C. S. (1984). *Interpersonal psychotherapy of depression.* New York, NY: Basic Books.

Kovacs, M., Rush, A. J., Beck, A. T., & Hollon, S. D. (1981). Depressed outpatients treated with cognitive therapy or pharmacotherapy. A one-year follow-up. *Archives of General Psychiatry, 38,* 33–39.

Kuyken, W., Byford, S., Taylor, R. D., Watkins, E., Holden, E., White, K., . . . Teasdale, J. D. (2008). Mindfulness-based cognitive therapy to prevent relapse in recurrent depression. *Journal of Consulting and Clinical Psychology, 76,* 966–978. doi:10.1037/a0013786

Kuyken, W., Fothergill, C. D., Musa, M., & Chadwick, P. (2005). The reliability and quality of cognitive case formulation. *Behaviour Research and Therapy, 43,* 1187–1201. doi:10.1016/j.brat.2004.08.007

Lavender, A., & Schmidt, U. (2006). Cognitive–behavioural case formulation in complex eating disorders. In N. Tarrier (Ed.), *Case formulation in cognitive behavioural therapy* (pp. 238–262). New York, NY: Routledge.

Leahy, R. L. (2001). *Overcoming resistance in cognitive therapy.* New York, NY: Guilford Press.

Leahy, R. L. (2003). *Cognitive therapy techniques: A practitioner's guide*. New York, NY: Guilford Press.

Lee, C. W., Taylor, G., & Dunn, J. (1999). Factor structure of the schema questionnaire in a large clinical sample. *Cognitive Therapy and Research, 23*, 441–451. doi:10.1023/A:1018712202933

Linehan, M. M. (1993). *Cognitive–behavioral treatment of borderline personality disorder*. New York, NY: Guilford Press.

Luborsky, L., & DeRubeis, R. J. (1984). The use of psychotherapy treatment manuals: A small revolution in psychotherapy research style. *Clinical Psychology Review, 4*, 5–14. doi:10.1016/0272-7358(84)90034-5

Ma, S. H., & Teasdale, J. D. (2004). Mindfulness-based cognitive therapy for depression: Replication and exploration of differential relapse prevention effects. *Journal of Consulting and Clinical Psychology, 72*, 31–40. doi:10.1037/0022-006X.72.1.31

Mahoney, M. J. (1974). *Cognition and behavior modification*. Cambridge, MA: Ballinger.

Mahoney, M. J. (1977). Personal science: A cognitive learning therapy. In A. Ellis & R. Greiger (Eds.), *Handbook of rational-emotive therapy* (pp. 352–368). New York, NY: Springer.

Mahoney, M. J. (1991). *Human change processes: The scientific foundations of psychotherapy*. New York, NY: Basic Books.

Martell, C. R., Safren, S. A., & Prince, S. E. (2004). *Cognitive–behavioral therapies with lesbian, gay, and bisexual clients*. New York, NY: Guilford Press.

McHugh, R. K., & Barlow, D. H. (2010). The dissemination and implementation of evidence-based psychological treatments: A review of current efforts. *American Psychologist, 65*, 73–84. doi:10.1037/a0018121

McMullin, R. E. (2000). *The new handbook of cognitive therapy techniques*. New York, NY: Norton.

Meichenbaum, D. (1977). *Cognitive–behavior modification*. New York, NY: Plenum Press.

Meichenbaum, D. H., & Deffenbacher, J. L. (1988). Stress inoculation training. *The Counseling Psychologist, 16*, 69–90. doi:10.1177/0011000088161005

Meichenbaum, D. H., & Jaremko, M. (Eds.). (1983). *Stress management and prevention: A cognitive–behavioral perspective*. New York, NY: Plenum Press.

Messer, S. B. (2004). Evidence-based practice: Beyond empirically supported treatments. *Professional Psychology: Research and Practice, 35*, 580–588. doi:10.1037/0735-7028.35.6.580

Neimeyer, R. A. (1995). Constructivist psychotherapies: Features, foundations, and future directions. In R. A. Neimeyer & M. J. Mahoney (Eds.), *Constructivism in psychotherapy* (pp. 11–38). Washington, DC: American Psychological Association. doi:10.1037/10170-001

Nezu, A. M., & Nezu, C. M. (2008). *Evidence-based outcome research: A practical guide for conducting randomized controlled trials for psychosocial interventions.* New York, NY: Oxford University Press.

Nezu, A. M., Nezu, C. M., & Lombardo, E. (2004). *Cognitive–behavioral case formulation and treatment design: A problem-solving approach.* New York, NY: Springer.

Norcross, J. C., Hedges, M., & Prochaska, J. O. (2002). The face of 2010: A Delphi poll on the future of psychotherapy. *Professional Psychology: Research and Practice, 33,* 316–322. doi:10.1037/0735-7028.33.3.316

O'Donohue, W., & Fisher, J. E. (Eds.). (2008). *Cognitive behavior therapy: Applying empirically supported techniques in your practice* (2nd ed.). New York, NY: Wiley.

O'Donohue, W. T., & Fisher, J. E. (2009). *General principles and empirically supported techniques of cognitive behavior therapy.* New York, NY: Wiley.

Olinger, L. J., Kuiper, N. A., & Shaw, B. F. (1987). Dysfunctional attitudes and stressful life events: An interactive model of depression. *Cognitive Therapy and Research, 11,* 25–40. doi:10.1007/BF01183130

Pantalone, D. W., Iwamasa, G. Y., & Martell, C. R. (2010). Cognitive–behavioral therapy with diverse populations. In K. S. Dobson (Ed.), *Handbook of cognitive–behavioral therapies* (3rd ed., pp. 445–464). New York, NY: Guilford Press.

Persons, J. B. (1989). *Cognitive therapy in practice: A case formulation approach.* New York, NY: Norton.

Persons, J. B. (1997). *Cognitive–behavioral case formulation.* Calgary, Alberta, Canada: Psychologists Association of Alberta.

Persons, J. B. (2008). *The case formulation approach to cognitive–behavior therapy.* New York, NY: Guilford Press.

Persons, J. B., & Davidson, J. (2010). Cognitive–behavioral case formulation. In K. S. Dobson (Ed.), *Handbook of cognitive–behavioral therapies* (3rd ed., pp. 172–196). New York, NY: Guilford Press.

Piaget, J. (1954). *The construction of reality in the child.* New York, NY: Ballantine Books. doi:10.1037/11168-000

Piaget, J. (1971). *Biology and knowledge.* Chicago, IL: University of Chicago Press.

Raghavan, C., Le, H., & Berenbaum, H. (2002). Predicting dysphoria and hostility using the diathesis–stress model of sociotropy and autonomy in a contextualized stress setting. *Cognitive Therapy and Research, 26,* 231–244. doi:10.1023/A:1014525920767

Rasmussen, P. R. (2005). *Personality-guided cognitive–behavioral therapy.* Washington, DC: American Psychological Association. doi:10.1037/11159-000

Reinecke, M. A., & Simmons, A. (2005). Vulnerability to depression among adolescents: Implications for cognitive–behavioral treatment. *Cognitive and Behavioral Practice, 12,* 166–176. doi:10.1016/S1077-7229(05)80022-7

Riso, L., du Toit, P. L., Stein, D. J., & Young, J. E. (Eds.). (2007). *Cognitive schemas and core beliefs in psychological problems: A scientist–practitioner guide.* Washington, DC: American Psychological Association. doi:10.1037/11561-000

Robins, C. J., Bagby, R. M., Rector, N. A., Lynch, T. R., & Kennedy, S. H. (1997). Sociotropy, autonomy, and patterns of symptoms in patients with major depression: A comparison of dimensional and categorical approaches. *Cognitive Therapy and Research, 21,* 285–300. doi:10.1023/A:1021874415967

Robins, C. J., & Block, P. (1989). Cognitive theories of depression viewed from a diathesis–stress perspective: Evaluations of the models of Beck and of Abramson, Seligman, and Teasdale. *Cognitive Therapy and Research, 13,* 297–313. doi:10.1007/BF01173475

Ross, L. R., & Clark, D. A. (1993). *A psychometric revision of Beck's Sociotropy–Autonomy Scale.* Poster session presented at the Annual Meeting of the Canadian Psychological Association, Montreal, Canada.

Rush, A. J., Beck, A. T., Kovacs, M., & Hollon, S. (1977). Comparative efficacy of cognitive therapy and pharmacotherapy in the treatment of depressed outpatients. *Cognitive Therapy and Research, 1*(1), 17–37. doi:10.1007/BF01173502

Safran, J. D. (1998). *Widening the scope of cognitive therapy: The therapeutic relationship, emotion and the process of change.* Northvale, NJ: Jason Aronson.

Safran, J. D., & Muran, C. (2000). *Negotiating the therapeutic alliance.* New York, NY: Guilford Press.

Sahin, N. H., & Sahin, N. (1992). How dysfunctional are the dysfunctional attitudes in another culture? *The British Journal of Medical Psychology, 65,* 17–26.

Salkovskis, P. M. (1989). Cognitive–behavioral factors and the persistence of intrusive thoughts in obsessional problems. *Behaviour Research and Therapy, 27,* 677–682. doi:10.1016/0005-7967(89)90152-6

Schmidt, N. B., Joiner, T. E., Young, J. E., & Telch, M. J. (1995). The Schema Questionnaire: Investigation of psychometric properties and the hierarchical structure of a measure of maladaptive schemas. *Cognitive Therapy and Research, 19,* 295–322. doi:10.1007/BF02230402

Segal, Z. V., Williams, J. M. G., & Teasdale, J. D. (2002). *Mindfulness-based cognitive therapy for depression.* New York, NY: Guilford Press.

Shapiro, J. R., Berkman, N. D., Brownley, K. A., Sedaway, J. A., Lohr, K. N., & Bulik, C. M. (2007). Bulimia nervosa treatment: A systematic review of randomized controlled trials. *International Journal of Eating Disorders, 40,* 321–336. doi:10.1002/eat.20372

Sholomskas, D. E., Syracuse-Siewert, G., Rounsaville, B. J., Ball, S. A., Nuro, K. F., & Carroll, K. M. (2005). We don't train in vain: A dissemination trial of three strategies of training clinicians in cognitive–behavioral therapy. *Journal of Consulting and Clinical Psychology, 73,* 106–115. doi:10.1037/0022-006X.73.1.106

Sotsky, S. M., Glass, D. R., Shea, M. T., Pilkonis, P. A., Collins, J. F., Elkin, I., . . . Oliveri, M. E. (1991). Patient predictors of response to psychotherapy and pharmacotherapy: Findings in the NIMH treatment of depression collaborative research program. *The American Journal of Psychiatry, 148,* 997–1008.

Strauman, T. J., & Higgins, E. T. (1993). The self construct in social cognition: Past, present and future. In Z. V. Segal & S. J. Blatt (Eds.), *The self in emotional distress: Cognitive and psychodynamic perspectives* (pp. 3–40). New York, NY: Guilford Press.

Strunk, D. R., & DeRubeis, R. J. (2001). Cognitive therapy for depression: A review of its efficacy. *Journal of Cognitive Psychotherapy, 15,* 289–297.

Tarrier, N. (Ed.). (2006). *Case formulation in cognitive behaviour therapy.* New York, NY: Routledge.

Weissman, A., & Beck, A. T. (1978). *Development and validation of the Dysfunctional Attitudes Scale: A preliminary investigation.* Paper presented at the annual meeting of the American Educational Research Association, Toronto, Ontario, Canada.

Weissman, M. M., Verdeli, H., Gameroff, M. J., Bledsoe, S. E., Betts, K., Mufson, L., . . . Wickramaratne, P. (2006). National survey of psychotherapy training in psychiatry, psychology, and social work. *Archives of General Psychiatry, 63,* 925–934. doi:10.1001/archpsyc.63.8.925

Welburn, K., Coristine, M., Dagg, P., Pontefract, A., & Jordan, S. (2002). The schema questionnaire—short form: Factor analysis and relationship between schemas and symptoms. *Cognitive Therapy and Research, 26,* 519–530. doi:10.1023/A:1016231902020

Wells, A. (2002). Worry, metacognition, and GAD: Nature, consequences, and treatment. *Journal of Cognitive Psychotherapy, 16,* 179–192. doi:10.1891/jcop.16.2.179.63994

Wells, A. (2006). Cognitive therapy case formulation in anxiety disorders. In N. Tarrier (Ed.), *Case formulation in cogntive behavior therapy* (pp. 52–80). New York, NY: Routledge.

Wells, A., & Sembi, S. (2004). Metacognitive therapy for PTSD: A core treatment manual. *Cognitive and Behavioral Practice, 11,* 365–377. doi:10.1016/S1077-7229(04)80053-1

Whittal, M. L., Agras, W. S., & Gould, R. A. (1999). Bulimia nervosa: A meta-analysis of psychosocial and pharmacological treatments. *Behavior Therapy, 30,* 117–135. doi:10.1016/S0005-7894(99)80049-5

Williams, J. M. G., Teasdale, J. D., Segal, Z. V., & Kabat-Zinn, J. (2007). *The mindful way through depression: Freeing yourself from chronic unhappiness.* New York, NY: Guilford Press.

Wolpe, J. (1969). *The practice of behavior therapy.* New York, NY: Pergamon Press.

Woody, S., & Rachman, S. (1994). Generalized anxiety disorder (GAD) as an unsuccessful search for safety. *Clinical Psychology Review, 14,* 743–753. doi:10.1016/0272-7358(94)90040-X

Young, J. E. (1990). *Cognitive therapy for personality disorders.* Sarasota, FL: Professional Resources Press.

Young, J. E., & Klosko, J. S. (1994). *Reinventing your life.* New York, NY: Plume.

Young, J. E., Klosko, J. S., & Weishaar, M. E. (2003). *Schema therapy: A practioner's guide.* New York, NY: Guilford Press.

Zajonc, R. B. (1980). Feeling and thinking. Preferences need no inferences. *American Psychologist, 35,* 151–175. doi:10.1037/0003-066X.35.2.151

Index

About the Author

Keith S. Dobson, PhD, is a professor of clinical psychology at the University of Calgary. He has served in various roles there, including past director of clinical psychology and co-leader of the Hotchkiss Brain Institute Depression Research program and head of psychology. His research focuses on cognitive models and mechanisms in depression and the treatment of depression, particularly with respect to cognitive–behavioral therapies.

He has published more than 150 articles and chapters and nine books and has given numerous conference and workshop presentations in many countries. Recent books include *The Prevention of Anxiety and Depression* (Dozois & Dobson, 2004), *Risk Factors for Depression* (Dobson & Dozois, 2008), *Evidence-Based Practice of Cognitive–Behavioral Therapy* (Dobson & Dobson, 2009), and the *Handbook of Cognitive–Behavioral Therapy* (3rd ed., Dobson, 2010).

In addition, he has written about developments in professional psychology and ethics and has been actively involved in organized psychology in Canada, including a term as president of the Canadian

Psychological Association. He was a member of the University of Calgary Research Ethics Board for many years and is past-president of both the Academy of Cognitive Therapy and the International Association for Cognitive Psychotherapy.

Among other awards, he received the Canadian Psychological Association's Award for Distinguished Contributions to the Profession of Psychology.

About the Series Editors

Jon Carlson, PsyD, EdD, ABPP, is distinguished professor of psychology and counseling at Governors State University in University Park, Illinois, and a psychologist at the Wellness Clinic in Lake Geneva, Wisconsin. Dr. Carlson has served as the editor of several periodicals, including the *Journal of Individual Psychology* and *The Family Journal.* He holds diplomas in both family psychology and Adlerian psychology. He has authored 150 journal articles and 40 books, including *Time for a Better Marriage, Adlerian Therapy, The Mummy at the Dining Room Table, Bad Therapy, The Client Who Changed Me,* and *Moved by the Spirit.* He has created more than 200 professional trade videos and DVDs with leading professional therapists and educators. In 2004 the American Counseling Association named him a "Living Legend." Recently he syndicated an advice cartoon, *On The Edge,* with cartoonist Joe Martin.

Matt Englar-Carlson, PhD, is a professor of counseling at California State University–Fullerton. He is a fellow of Division 51 of the American Psychological Association (APA). As a scholar, teacher, and clinician, Dr. Englar-Carlson has been an innovator and professionally passionate about training and teaching clinicians to work more effectively with their male clients. He has more than 30 publications and 50 national and international presentations, most of which are focused on men and masculinity and diversity issues in psychological training and practice. Dr. Englar-Carlson coedited the books *In the Room With Men: A Casebook of Therapeutic Change* and *Counseling Troubled Boys: A Guidebook for Professionals* and was featured in the 2010 APA-produced DVD *Engaging Men in Psychotherapy*. In 2007, he was named Researcher of the Year by the Society for the Psychological Study of Men and Masculinity. He is also a member of the APA Working Group to Develop Guidelines for Psychological Practice With Boys and Men. As a clinician, he has worked with children, adults, and families in school, community, and university mental health settings.